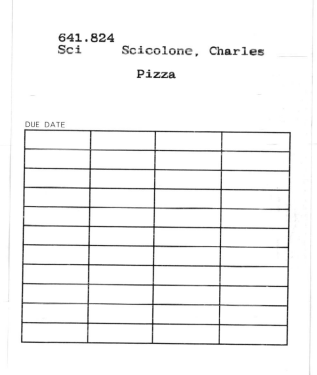

pizza

any way you slice it

MARINARA con vongole
Aglio, Origano, Pomodoro e Prezzemolo
MARGHERITA
Pomodoro, Mozzarella, Formaggio e Basilico
MARGHERITA con uovo
Pomodoro, Mozzarella, Formaggio e Basilico
MARGHERITA con prosciutto
Pomodoro, Mozzarella, Formaggio e Basilico
MARGHERITA con funghi
Pomodoro, Mozzarella, Formaggio e Basilico
MARGHERITA alla romana
Mozzarella, Acciughe, Pomodoro e Basilico
MARGHERITA con prosciutto e funghi
Pomodoro, Mozzarella, Formaggio e Basilico
MARGHERITA con panna
Pomodoro, Mozzarella, Formaggio, Basilico e Panna
MARGHERITA con filetto pomodorini
Filetto di pomodoro, Fior di latte, Formaggio e Basilico
PIZZA al prosciutto crudo
Pomodoro, Mozzarella, Prosciutto crudo,
Formaggio e Basilico
PIZZA CAPRESE
Pomodoro per insalata, Mozzarella, Basilico ed Origano
PIZZA alla campagnola
Olive, Acciughe, Pomodoro, Capperi, Aglio ed Origano
PIZZA sostanziosa
Pomodoro, Mozzarella, Prosciutto, Uovo,
Formaggio e Basilico
PIZZA lasagna
Pomodoro, Mozzarella, Ricotta, Prosciutto, Formaggio e
PIZZA forte
Salame piccante, Peperoni sottolio, Pomodoro,
Peperoncino e Basilico
PIZZA alle 4 stagioni

OTEL SANTA LUCIA
NAPOLI

pizza

any way you slice it

charles and michele scicolone

BROADWAY BOOKS / NEW YORK

Pizzeria TRIAN

NAPOLI - Via Pietro Colletta n. 42/44/46
Tel. (081) 553.94.26

ORDINAZIONE N. 0290   TAVOLO N.

MARINARA
Aglio, Origano, Pomodoro e Basilico
MARINARA con vongole
Aglio, Origano, Pomodoro e Prezzemolo
MARGHERITA
Pomodoro, Mozzarella, Formaggio e Basilico
MARGHERITA con uova
Pomodoro, Mozzarella, Formaggio e Basilico
MARGHERITA con prosciutto
Pomodoro, Mozzarella, Formaggio e Basilico
MARGHERITA con funghi
Pomodoro, Mozzarella, Formaggio e Basilico
MARGHERITA alla romana
Mozzarella, Acciughe, Pomodoro e Basilico
MARGHERITA con prosciutto e funghi
Pomodoro, Mozzarella, Formaggio e Basilico
MARGHERITA con panna
Pomodoro, Mozzarella, Formaggio e Panna
MARGHERITA con filetto pomodorini
Filetto di pomodoro, Fior di latte, Formaggio e Basilico
PIZZA al prosciutto crudo
Pomodoro, Mozzarella, Prosciutto crudo,
Formaggio e Basilico

Broadway Books titles may be purchased for business or promotional use or for special sales. For information, please write to: Special Markets Department, Bantam Doubleday Dell Publishing Group, Inc., 1540 Broadway, New York, NY 10036.

BROADWAY BOOKS and its logo, a letter B bisected on the diagonal, are trademarks of Broadway Books, a division of Bantam Doubleday Dell Publishing Group, Inc.

Some of the recipes in this collection appeared in different form in *McCall's*, *Gourmet*, *Eating Well*, and *Great American Home Cooking*.

Library of Congress Cataloging-in-Publication Data
Scicolone, Charles.
    Pizza : any way you slice it / Charles and Michele Scicolone.—1st ed.
      p.   cm.
    Includes bibliographical references and index.
    ISBN 0-7679-0147-9
    1. Pizza.   I. Scicolone, Michele.   II. Title.
TX770.P58S25   1998
641.8′24—dc21   98-14357
                                                                 CIP

FIRST EDITION
Designed by Barbara Balch
Photographs by Ellen Silverman
98 99 00 01 02 10 9 8 7 6 5 4 3 2 1

ah, the pizza! Something bitter and sweet, long and short, old and new, always the same yet totally unexpected, the staff of life and its incomparable accompaniment! I have a special liking for this poor man's dish which is as rich in symbols as the sacred host. While you are eating a pizza you can tell it all your troubles, how far behind you are on your rent, how you lost your job, with whom you have transacted some slightly unsavory piece of business, or anything else you like. No other dish is as companionable; the pizza is a moon on your plate and no matter how deep may be the night of your appetite, it will always light up the way.

GIUSEPPE MORATTA

contents

pizza

any way you slice it

S·AGLIERA

Brandi®
La pizza... dal 1780

EL SANTA LUCIA
NAPOLI

introduction

$\mathcal{W}$e never set out to write a book about pizza; it just happened. A few years ago Michele went to southern Italy on a trip organized by the International Olive Oil Council. The first stop was Naples, and though her stay there was brief, she came back full of descriptions of the city's wonders—the setting, the people, the music. The food was fantastic and the pizza was the best she had ever tasted. Charles was not convinced—after all, he had eaten his share of fine pizzas all over Italy, but Michele obviously was enchanted and longed to return. Since we had not been to Naples together in more than twenty years, it seemed like a good idea.

We visit Italy at least two or three times a year, for business, for pleasure, and just because we love it. We decided to include Naples in our next itinerary, planning that if it proved disappointing, we could always go back to Rome. Naples, though, was anything but disappointing. In fact, it far exceeded our expectations. We love big cities, and this one has all the qualities we look for—and then some. "See Naples and die," said Goethe, and it is as true now as it was then.

The views, with the broad sweep of the Bay of Naples, Vesuvius in the distance, palm trees, and baroque architecture, are incomparable. We walked everywhere and looked at everything, tasted everything. And Charles was gripped by a pizza frenzy. After his first pizza at Ciro a Santa Brigida, one of the city's great restaurants, he was unstoppable. He ate pizza everywhere, several times a day, in restaurants or from take-out places while we walked around the city.

When we returned home, Charles had only one question. Where can we get pizza like we ate in Naples? Michele jokingly replied, make it yourself.

Until that trip, we had thought that, as knowledgeable Italian travelers and New Yorkers, we knew all about good pizza. But Neapolitan pizza is different from pizza anywhere else. Each pie is hand shaped so that it has a natural look. Baked in wood-burning ovens, the crusts are blistered and even slightly charred with a wonderful smoky flavor. The crusts are thin, though not too thin, perfectly balanced between crispness and chewiness. Toppings are light and intensely flavorful. Everyone gets his or her own pie.

Charles set out to duplicate those unforgettable Neapolitan pizzas in our home kitchen. We should explain that this was a pretty incredible notion. Charles was infamous for never having cooked a thing in his entire life. He had never made so much as a pot of coffee or scrambled an egg. Until our trip to Naples, he would never even think of making himself a meal or even reheating takeout food.

Michele decided to humor him and gave him some cookbooks to read on how to make pizza and bread dough. With a little guidance, he began to experiment. He had to learn everything—the difference between a teaspoon and a tablespoon, how to measure flour and water correctly, and to dissolve yeast. Soon he was reading everything he could about pizza ingredients. He began hanging out in pizza parlors, watching the *pizzaioli* at their work, tasting their pizza, and asking questions. Motivated by his love for Neapolitan pizza and the difficulty of finding it, he was determined to prove that good Neapolitan-style pizza could be made at home. Charles made pizza after pizza, each one a little better than the one that preceded it.

You never know how many friends you have until you start making pizza. Skeptics, who had heard about Charles's passion for pizza, began clamoring to taste his pies. They were amazed at how good they were, and at how Charles, who had never cooked anything in his life, was able to make pizza from scratch all by himself.

Based on the premise that if he could do it, it must be easy, our friends began to ask Charles to show them how to make pizza. He was delighted to share his newfound ability, reinforcing his knowledge by methodically explaining his techniques to others. Michele, too, became involved in making pizza—after all, the kitchen is usually her domain. Together we continued to experiment and improve our pies. Everyone said, why don't you two write a book about pizza.

Researching techniques and varieties brought us to a greater appreciation of the foods that fit into the category of pizza. Friends and relatives reminded us of the traditional pizzas they had made or tasted. Several shared treasured family recipes and directed us to good pizzerias. Pizza makers both here and in Italy gave us tips and hints.

Our friend Nicola Marzovilla, owner of New York's i Trulli Restaurant and Enoteca, allowed us to use the restaurant's wood-fired oven to bake our pies. When *Vanity Fair* magazine organized a party at the restaurant to celebrate the publication of General Colin Powell's book, they insisted on having pizza at the cocktail hour. Nicola knew where to turn for an expert pizzaiolo. Charles turned out his delicious pies for the general and many of his celebrity friends and for the media.

We wrote articles about pizza making for several magazines, including *McCall's, Gourmet, Great American Home Cooking,* and *Eating Well.* We taught pizza-making classes at numerous cooking schools around the country. Little by little, and quite naturally, our recipe repertoire grew and grew and this book began to take shape.

Like most people, we do not have a wood-fired oven at home, so our goal with this book has been to develop recipes for the best possible pizza that can be made in an ordinary household oven. We have both a gas and an electric oven in our kitchen and tested these recipes in both. Made with the finest fresh ingredients and eaten hot out of the oven in the comfort of home, our pizzas are as good as they get!

Here, then, is a collection of recipes and information about making many kinds of pizza, not just Neapolitan-style but contemporary American-style pizzas, unique filled pizzas, regional Italian pizzas, and focaccias—something for every taste. Follow our instructions, don't be afraid to experiment, and soon you, too, will be making terrific pizza. It really is not difficult, and it is a lot of fun for the whole family. Remember, if Charles can make great pizza, anyone can.

OTEL SANTA LUCIA
NAPOLI

ingredients and equipment

anchovies/

People either love or hate canned anchovies—they rarely take the middle ground. We are firmly planted in the former group, especially when we can find anchovies packed in salt, which have a richer flavor than anchovies packed in oil.

Of the oil-packed varieties, buy the kind that come in little jars rather than small flat cans so you can see if the anchovies are plump and meaty, or old and crumbly before you buy them. The jars are resealable, so if you do not use all the anchovies at one time, you can save them easily. If you do have leftover oil-packed anchovies, transfer them to a small glass jar, if necessary, and cover them with the oil they were packed in or with fresh olive oil. Use them up as quickly as possible, since once the container is opened, anchovies soon develop an off taste.

Don't buy the canned rolled anchovies wrapped around capers. They are meant to be a garnish, not a cooking ingredient.

Salt-packed anchovies can be purchased in one-pound cans, or you may be able to buy a smaller amount from a larger can at some markets. To prepare salted anchovies, rinse as many as you need under cool running water. Pull the two fillets apart with your fingers and discard the bony central frame. Rinse again and pat dry. The anchovies are ready to use. They can be eaten as is or used for cooking. Keep the remaining anchovies in the refrigerator, covered with coarse salt and a layer of plastic wrap.

basil/

The heat from a baked pizza is enough to coax a mouthwatering aroma from a few leaves of fresh basil. For a touch of color and enhanced flavor and aroma scatter some over the sizzling pie as it emerges from the oven. During the summer we have a big pot of basil growing in the backyard or we buy it at our local greengrocers. We put it in a jar of water and keep it on the kitchen counter for a couple of days, changing the water daily. Refrigerated basil tends to blacken quickly from the cold. It helps a little if you wrap the top of the bunch in paper towels and a plastic bag and keep it in the warmest spot on the lowest shelf of the refrigerator.

We also keep a plastic bag full of rinsed, dried basil leaves in the freezer for emergencies. Though frozen basil is too soggy when thawed to use in salads, it is fine added to cooked foods like tomato sauces and on pizza. Dried basil, like dried parsley does not have much flavor and we never use it. Use dried oregano, if you have no fresh or frozen basil and want an herbal flavor. Dried oregano does not taste the same, but it is nonetheless very good.

cheeses/

asiago/ Asiago is a cow's milk cheese that takes its name from a small town in the Veneto region of northeastern Italy. It is semifirm and flavorful but not too sharp or spicy. Asiago slices well and melts beautifully, so it is also good cheese for topping pizza.

mozzarella/ In Naples mozzarella means *mozzarella di bufala,* a fresh, tasty cheese made from the milk of water buffaloes. No one is quite sure how these enormous, ungainly-looking beasts found their way to Italy, but they have been raised in the area south of Rome for centuries. The animal's milk is prized for its richness—it has about 50 percent more protein and twice as much fat (7 to 9 percent) as whole cow's milk, though water buffalo milk is lower in saturated fat.

Mozzarella made from cow's milk is called *fior di latte*, flower of the milk. Though not as flavorful as mozzarella di bufala, it is still very good-tasting. Buffalo milk mozzarella is expensive, and some pizza makers feel that it is better appreciated on its own, not melted on a pizza. Both are sold swimming in whey and are juicy when cut.

The technique for making mozzarella is simple. First, the milk is heated to about 100°F, then rennet and a starter culture are stirred in. The milk is left to coagulate and form a curd. After about an hour and a half, the curd is broken up, releasing the whey, the liquid part of the milk, which is drawn off to be used to make ricotta. The curds are then mixed with very hot water and stirred until they become stringy like soft taffy. Finally the cheesemaker cuts off—*mozzare* in Italian—hunks of the cheese and shapes them into balls. The balls are placed in lightly salted water to cool and set. Because of the stringy, layered texture of mozzarella, it is called a *pasta filata*, or stringy dough cheese.

When we make pizza at home, we generally use fresh cow's milk mozzarella. We are fortunate to live in an area where we can buy mozzarella made fresh daily. It has a sweet creamy flavor and melts beautifully, though it is hard to resist slicing it up and eating it without any cooking. Though more readily available here than it once was, buffalo mozzarella is still not easy to find, so we don't use it all that often.

Fresh mozzarella is at its best when just made. A cold refrigerator makes it turn rubbery so, if possible, buy it and use it as soon as possible. If it is too watery, blot the slices dry before putting them on pizza. Fresh mozzarella is too soft to grate, so we cut it into slices. For a less solid topping, tear the slices into three or four pieces. If fresh mozzarella is not available in your area, consider ordering it from one of the mail order sources listed in the back of this book.

All too often, pizza makers in this country use "pizza cheese," a product specially formulated for pizzerias that becomes dry and stringy when cooked. Not much better is the hard, salty mozzarella sold in supermarkets. Both have little in common with fresh mozzarella. If you do use one of these hard, dry cheeses, bury it under the sauce, instead of placing it on top, so that the cheese will be less plasticlike when it melts. Low-fat

homemade mozzarella

makes about 1 pound

1 ½ **pounds cheese curd**

1. Fill two large bowls with cold water. Add ice if necessary. Fill a third large bowl with very hot but not scalding tap water. Place the cheese curd in the hot water. Dip your hands in the cold water to chill them. Plunge your hands into the hot water and begin pressing and squeezing the curd, keeping it under water. Handle the cheese very, very gently or it will toughen. When your hands feel hot, dip them in the cool water, then return to massaging the cheese in the hot water. When the water cools down, drain it off and add fresh hot water. Repeat massaging the curd, stretching the outside skin of the curd and molding it into a ball, until the cheese is soft and malleable. Change the water at least one more time.

2. When the cheese is very soft, begin to shape it into smaller balls about 2 inches in diameter called *bocconcini,* little mouthfuls, by squeezing a small amount between your thumb and forefinger. Give the ball a twist, then pinch it off. Round the ball by holding it in your hands, palms outstretched, and rotating it clockwise, stretching the skin and smoothing it. Dip the ball in the hot water periodically to keep it warm and soft. Do not overwork the curd. Place the finished ball in the cold water to set. Repeat with the remaining curd, making large or small balls as desired. The mozzarella will firm up slightly as it cools. It is ready to eat immediately or it can be held at cool room temperature for up to 1 hour. For longer storage, place the mozzarella in the refrigerator in an airtight container covered with fresh cold water. The mozzarella keeps for several days, though it is best eaten at room temperature.

To shape the mozzarella into knots, break off a piece of cheese and gently squeeze and stretch it to form a rope about ¾ inch thick. Tie the rope into a knot near the cut end. Tighten the knot by pulling it toward the tip. Cut the rope just below the knot and repeat. Drop the shaped knots into the cold water to firm up.

mozzarella, like most low-fat cheeses, is tasteless and not worth eating. If you are watching your fat intake, forget the cheese and make simple, delicious pizza marinara instead.

If you like, you can make your own fresh mozzarella at home (see recipe page 10). It is fun and not difficult to do—the only problem is obtaining the cheese curd. Making your own curd is not impossible, but you would need such large quantities of milk that it is not practical. Most shops that make and sell fresh mozzarella buy their curd from large commercial suppliers. Some shops will sell you the cheese curd, but many prefer to sell you the cheese for which they can ask a higher price. In our neighborhood, we can buy mozzarella cheese curd at our local Fratelli Pasta store. They make lovely fresh mozzarella all day, but the manager, Luciano, is nice enough to sell us the curd whenever we want some. You can also order fresh mozzarella curd by mail from Balducci's (see page 201).

ricotta/ In Italy ricotta is a by-product of the production of hard aged cheeses like Parmigiano-Reggiano, pecorino Romano, and provolone. To make these cheeses, the *casaro,* or cheesemaker, adds rennet or a similar product to the fresh milk, which can be either cow, sheep, goat, or water buffalo, depending on the type of cheese. Then the cheesemaker heats the rennet-milk mixture, which causes the protein in the milk to coagulate and separate from the whey and form curds. The curds are pressed and aged to make hard cheeses, while the whey, the watery part of the milk, remains to be made into ricotta. The cheesemaker cooks the whey again—hence the name *ricotta*—and the small amount of protein left in the liquid coagulates to form ricotta. In Italy ricotta is not considered a cheese, but a dairy product.

Ricotta made at home is a little different from the kind described here, but it is easy to do and the flavor is so fresh and good that once you try it, you will find all kinds of ways to use it (see recipe page 13). We serve it as an appetizer, drizzled with fresh herbs, garlic, olive oil, and pepper, or for dessert, drizzled with honey and chopped walnuts. It is delicious spread on breakfast toast, sprinkled with sugar and cinnamon, or topped with preserves. Of course, it is excellent as a stuffing or topping for all kinds of pizzas.

fontina/ Fontina is a semifirm cow's milk cheese that is made in many different countries. The best comes from the Valle d'Aosta region in northwestern Italy, near the Swiss border. Aged in deep mountain caves, Fontina Valle d'Aosta has a mild but full, rich flavor and a natural reddish golden brown rind. We consider it one of the best eating cheeses there is. Since it melts beautifully, Fontina is also perfect for pizza and other cooked dishes.

parmigiano-reggiano/ If we could have only one cheese for cooking and eating, our choice would be easy—Parmigiano-Reggiano. This firm, nutty, crumbly cheese is completely different from the tasteless stuff you find in shakers at local pizzerias. Parmigiano-Reggiano is a cow's milk cheese that can only be produced in a limited area of northern Italy. It is made completely by hand and aged about eighteen months, so that it slowly develops its fine flavor. We always have a hunk of it in our refrigerator ready for grating on pizza, pasta, soup, and salads, or to use as a cooking ingredient, or to cut into small chunks for nibbling.

provolone/ A former student of ours was in Italy for the first time and decided to buy some fixings for a picnic. He stopped at a *salumeria* with a tempting display and ordered, among other items, some thinly sliced provolone. To his surprise, the counterman refused to give it to him. Our friend insisted, and the counterman became annoyed and refused again. Finally our friend, who did not understand Italian, gave up, thinking he had just encountered the rudest deli man in Italy. What he did not realize, until we explained it to him back home, was that genuine Italian provolone really cannot be sliced thin, since it is rather firm and tends to crumble when sliced. It is nothing like the kind of provolone we see most often here—thin-sliced sheets of bland, plasticlike cheese for sandwiches.

Italian provolone has a yellowish beige rind and a creamy interior. It is made from cow's milk and comes in different shapes, including round balls, melon shapes, and long sausage shapes, all bound with rope so that they can be hung from the rafters for aging. It ranges in flavor and texture from sharp and firm while young to very

homemade ricotta

makes about 1 cup

1 quart whole or low-fat milk
2 tablespoons fresh lemon juice,
strained, or ¹/₂ cup buttermilk

1. Moisten a large piece of cheesecloth and squeeze it dry. Line a large strainer with the cheesecloth and set it over a bowl.

2. In a medium saucepan, bring all the ingredients to a simmer. Cook over low heat, stirring once or twice, until the milk separates and large curds form, about 4 minutes. Pour the mixture into the strainer. Let stand until cooled and the liquid has stopped dripping, about 30 minutes.

3. Transfer to a covered container and refrigerate until ready to use. Fresh ricotta will keep up to 3 days.

sharp and crumbly when aged. It is great served with olives or marinated mushrooms (see recipe on page 180) as an antipasto or on certain pizzas, especially those that include eggplant and tomatoes among their ingredients.

taleggio/ In his comprehensive book *Cheese Primer* (Workman, 1997), Steve Jenkins calls creamy cow's milk Taleggio "northern Italy's best kept secret—the most refined and sophisticated of all Italian cheeses." We could not agree more. Soft and buttery, Taleggio is delicious and spreadable. It melts beautifully on pizza or tossed with pasta, or spread it on warm focaccia and serve with a salad.

crushed red pepper/

Peperoncini is the Italian name for red chilies. They are used sparingly in Italian cooking but have a major impact on the flavor of many pizzas. We buy tiny firey, dried chilies called *diavolicchi*, little devils, in Italy to crumble over pizzas or into sauces. Use crushed red pepper or red pepper flakes if you cannot find the whole chilies.

If you like, you can place some crumbled dried chilies or crushed red pepper in olive oil to make what the Italians call *olio santo*, or holy oil, for anointing a pizza. As it sits, the oil absorbs the flavor and heat from the chilies.

flour/

Flour made from wheat grown in North America has a high protein content because it is made from hard winter or spring wheat. High-protein flour, sold labeled as bread flour, is good for bread baking because it makes a crusty, chewy loaf, but it is too hard for pizza, which should not be as firm as bread.

When purchasing flour, buy it from a store that has a good turnover so that the flour you buy will be fresh. Don't buy more flour than you can use in a reasonable amount of time, about two or three months. At home, keep flour in an air-tight container in a cool dry place.

unbleached all-purpose flour/ This type of flour has a lower protein content than bread flour and when used for pizza dough makes an excellent crisp, firm, chewy, crust. Do not confuse it with all-purpose flour, which has been chemically whitened. We use unbleached all-purpose flour for making our American-style and filled pizzas and focaccias, or we blend it with cake flour for Neapolitan-style pizzas.

cake flour/ This type of flour is lower in protein than all-purpose flour and is usually used to make cakes and pastries with a soft, tender texture. We mix cake flour with unbleached all-purpose flour to create a flour blend that is similar to what Italian pizza makers use. This blended flour makes a very light pizza crust that is flexible, chewy, and crisp. We use it for our Neapolitan-style pizzas.

There are two kinds of cake flour: plain and self-rising. Do not use the self-rising type, which is blended with baking powder and salt.

semolina or semolina flour/ This is a fine to coarsely ground flour made from durum, a kind of hard wheat. During processing, the bran and germ of durum wheat grains are removed and the remainder, called the endosperm, is ground into a grainy type of flour. The flour has a light creamy yellow color and a gritty texture. In Sicily and other parts of southern Italy, semolina flour is used to make focaccia and stuffed pizza doughs as well as certain types of pasta. Semolina makes a very stiff dough, so it is usually combined with softer flours to make it more manageable.

Packaging labels are sometimes confusing, and semolina flour may be sold labeled as pasta flour, durum flour, fine or coarse semolina, or just semolina flour. For the recipes in this book, fine semolina flour is the one to use. It has the consistency of very fine sand. If you can only find a coarse-grain semolina, pour it into a food processor with a steel blade and grind it up until it is fine.

whole wheat flour/ This type of flour has a slightly coarse or gritty texture and beige color with light brown flecks. It is made by grinding up the whole wheat berry including the bran. Whole wheat flour is used in some pizza and focaccia recipes but it is always mixed with white flour or the dough would be too heavy. Whole wheat flour goes rancid quickly and should be stored in a tightly sealed plastic bag or container in the refrigerator or freezer.

garlic/

Fresh garlic adds great flavor to pizza and many other foods. Buy whole heads of garlic that are firm and white or purplish—the color depends on the variety of the garlic plant. Garlic that is not fresh will be sprouting at the tip, and the cloves may be yellowed or shriveled. Keep garlic cloves in an airy place at cool room temperature or in the crisper drawer of your refrigerator. Do not use dried garlic powder or flakes. Its flavor is sharp and sour and will detract from the goodness of your homemade pizza.

Never store fresh garlic—or any other plant product—under oil at room temperature unless it has been fully cooked or treated with ascorbic acid. There is always a danger of botulism poisoning. Even if it is refrigerated, garlic is best used within a day or two.

olive oil/

Our first bite of pizza at Gigino Pizza a Metro (also known as the Pizza University), an enormous restaurant in Vico Equense, near Naples, was a revelation. Though we had ordered a simple pizza margherita, our pie had a rich, meaty taste as if it were layered with prosciutto. We devoured it, speculating on where the meaty flavor was coming from. On our way out, we stopped to watch the pizzaiolo at work. Just before baking the pies, he would dip a ladle into a metal container on the counter and drizzle the contents over the pizzas. We asked him what it was and he told us it was *sugno*, lard. That explained the hammy flavor of our pizza!

At one time lard was the typical cooking fat used in Naples for topping pizzas and for most other cooking purposes, but today, health-conscious Italians are switching to olive oil. Now even Gigino's offers their customers a choice.

The flavor, price, and quality of olive oil vary considerably, so try several brands until you find one you like. Only olive oil with the finest flavor and lowest acid content is labeled extra virgin. We use extra virgin olive oil for most cooking purposes, and keep two or three kinds on hand. A supermarket brand is fine for cooking, but we reserve the better-quality oils for drizzling on soup, or for salad dressings. A drizzle of fine olive oil is a perfect finishing touch on a hot baked pizza.

When purchasing olive oil, don't buy more than you can use in a couple of months. Unlike wine, olive oil does not improve with age, so use it up as quickly as possible. Once the container is opened, olive oil deteriorates even more rapidly. Keep it in a cool, dark place. It will harden if it is refrigerated, but will quickly liquefy at room temperature. If the container is left open for a long period of time in a warm kitchen or under bright lights, the oil can go rancid, in which case it should be discarded.

prosciutto/

This type of unsmoked ham is made both here and in Italy. At its best, sliced prosciutto is a deep rose pink with a border of creamy white fat and a soft, silken texture. Unfortunately, some merchants do not handle it properly or do not sell it quickly enough. Even the finest quality prosciutto can be spoiled if it is too old, dried out, or badly sliced, so shop carefully.

Some of the finest prosciutto comes from Parma in Italy and is widely available here. The animals from which Prosciutto di Parma is made are fed on the whey that is left over from the making of Parmigiano-Reggiano. The hams are rubbed with seasonings and hung to dry slowly so that meat becomes moist and flavorful. Sliced Prosciutto di Parma has recently become available in sealed plastic containers so that it stays fresh and in perfect condition.

salt/

A friend of ours once recommended a New York pizzeria where the pizza makers all came from Naples. We tried the pizza there, but it was very disappointing. The crust was made without salt.

After we had eaten, we stopped to talk to the pizzaiolo. Since he asked us what we thought, we told him that the pizza needed salt. He seemed surprised and replied that Americans don't like salt, therefore he wasn't using any! He was misguided. Pizza dough without salt, or any unsalted bread, is bland and tasteless.

Kosher, coarse, and sea salts are preferable to table salt because they have a better flavor. Taste them side by side and compare. If you are accustomed to using fine table salt and switch to kosher, coarse, or sea salt, you may need to use more of the latter. The reason is that these salts are flakier and actually weigh less than the more compact table salts. If you buy coarse salt in large crystals, you will need to grind it in a salt mill or it may not melt completely in the dough.

tomatoes/

In Naples the tomatoes that go on a pizza are usually fresh, very ripe, and uncooked. Even in the winter, Italians like to use little fresh tomatoes, called *pomodori a pendolo,* or hanging tomatoes. They are about the size of cherry tomatoes and grow somewhat like grapes on a vine. As their season comes to an end, the whole vine is picked and hung up to dry in a cool place. The tomatoes get riper and somewhat drier as they age, but their flavor remains sweet. Usually the cook just crushes them with his hands and scatters them on top of a pizza or simmers them quickly into a sauce.

Once Michele tried to grow Neapolitan tomatoes in our Brooklyn backyard from seeds brought back from Italy. The plants grew, though the tomatoes were few and far between. September came and they showed no sign of ripening. She gave up one chilly morning when she discovered two squirrels having a feast—one shook the plants while the other devoured the hard green tomatoes.

When sweet, vine-ripened tomatoes are not available, Italians rely on canned San Marzano tomatoes, and so do we. San Marzano is a region near Mt. Vesuvius with soil and growing conditions that result in perfect tomatoes. They are picked and canned when they are fully ripe and just the right consistency to make good-tasting sauces. Different companies market San Marzano tomatoes in the United States under various brand names, but this does not mean that the tomatoes are genuine Italian San Marzanos. When you shop, look for the name "San Marzano" somewhere on the label, and the words "Product of Italy" in fine print.

Choose whole tomatoes—cans of crushed tomatoes often contain excessive amounts of seeds. Another advantage of whole tomatoes is that you can tell when you open the can if they were fully ripe when they were packed or still greenish and hard at the ends. Try several brands until you find one you like.

Because professional pizza ovens are so hot, Italian pizza makers do not use a cooked pizza sauce as we know it. If they did, the cooked sauce would become overcooked. Instead, they simply crush up the tomatoes—fresh or canned—and scatter them over the pizza. If they are a little too juicy, they simply drain them with a slotted spoon.

Since our home oven is not nearly as hot as a professional pizza oven, we do make a lightly cooked sauce for our pizzas, especially when using canned tomatoes. We feel that the cooking takes away the canned flavor of the tomatoes, sweetens them, and concentrates the flavor, much as a hot pizza oven would.

When fresh ripe tomatoes are available, we simply chop or crush them, drain them, and use them as is. Never refrigerate fresh tomatoes. Store them at room temperature. Cold temperatures cause tomatoes to lose their flavor and turn mushy.

water/

When the pizzeria Naples 45 opened in New York, the owners did everything to make authentic Neapolitan pizza, even importing the hard water for the dough from Naples. The costs soon became prohibitive, so they searched for a more convenient source of water with similar properties, reportedly settling on a site somewhere in Missouri.

The mineral and chemical content and flavor of water can adversely affect pizza dough. A high content of chlorine and fluoride can inhibit the action of the yeast. We recommend using purified water or bottled spring water.

Water temperature is very important when dissolving yeast. Very hot or cold water can damage yeast cells, so be sure to use water that is warm to the touch.

yeast/

Yeast is a microscopic member of the fungus family. In pizza dough, the activity of the yeast results in a light texture, good flavor, and tantalizing aroma.

All yeast is dormant when you buy it, but when mixed with flour and warm water, it comes alive and begins to feed on the sugars in the flour. As it feeds, the yeast expels carbon dioxide and alcohol in a process called fermentation. The escaping carbon dioxide becomes trapped in tiny pockets in the dough formed by the flour and water in the process of kneading. As the amount of carbon dioxide increases, it inflates the pockets and causes the dough to rise.

Yeast can be purchased in several forms. Most of the time we use active dry yeast for pizza. Active dry yeast is available in jars or in convenient premeasured $1/4$-ounce packages, usually sold in strips of three packages. Use scissors to separate the packages without tearing them open. About $2^1/2$ teaspoons of active dry yeast, the amount found in the premeasured packages, is enough to rise a dough made with 3 to 6 cups of flour.

If you bake a lot of pizza or bread, buy active dry yeast in jars, which are more economical than the premeasured packages. Once opened, a jar of yeast will be good for about six months if kept cool and dry. Be careful always to use a clean, dry measuring spoon and store the jar tightly closed in the freezer.

Since yeast cells are living organisms, they can die if stored incorrectly, overheated, or kept too long. If you are not sure what condition your yeast is in, you can "proof" it by mixing it with a teaspoon of sugar and the amount of warm water called for in the recipe. If the yeast gets foamy within a few minutes, it is viable and the mixture can be added to the flour. The small amount of sugar used for proofing will not noticeably affect the flavor of the dough. We generally skip this proofing step, since we frequently use up and replenish our yeast supply. However, it is a good precaution to take if you have yeast that is in doubtful condition. When purchasing yeast, check the expiration date on the package.

instant yeast/ A new type of yeast has become available to home bakers. Made from a different strain than that used for active dry yeast, instant yeast does not need to be dissolved in water before being added to the flour mixture, and it works in a wider temperature range than active dry yeast. Since it is stronger, you can use about 25 percent less instant yeast than active all-purpose yeast, or 2 teaspoons instant yeast in place of $2^1/2$ teaspoons (one $1/4$-ounce package) active dry yeast.

fast-acting yeast/ Don't confuse fast-acting yeast with instant yeast. Fast-acting yeast is a slightly different strain of yeast with thinner cell walls. It can be mixed with dry ingredients and does not have to be dissolved first in water. This type of yeast also tolerates higher temperatures and is treated with conditioners that make it work faster. Many bakers object to it because they feel that dough risen with fast-acting yeast does not develop the flavor and texture of dough that has risen more slowly. We rarely use it.

moist or cake yeast/ Sold in foil-wrapped cubes in the refrigerator section of some supermarkets, this is the type of yeast preferred by many bakers because it contains more active yeast cells than dried yeast. Unfortunately, it does not keep well and is not widely available. If you decide to use it, pay careful attention to the expiration date printed on the package. Proof fresh yeast as indicated on page 20 to be sure it is alive.

brewer's yeast/ Available in health stores, this yeast is a nutritional supplement that does not have any leavening properties. It is not meant to be added to dough.

equipment

dough scraper/

Made of thin plastic or metal, a dough or pastry scraper, also called a "bench knife," is terrific for lifting sticky doughs, scraping work surfaces for easy cleanup, and cutting a ball of dough into smaller pieces. We also use it for transferring chopped ingredients from cutting board to cooking pot. It is really like having an extra hand.

flour dredger/

We keep a large salt shaker filled with all-purpose flour handy for dusting the dough. Be sure to label the shaker carefully so as not to confuse it with salt or sugar.

metal spatula or pancake turner/

Buy the longest and widest metal spatula that you can find. It is useful for lifting hot pizza out of the oven. You could use your peel to remove the pizza, but the metal spatula is better if the pizza topping has melted and is sticking to the stone. We recommend two kinds of spatula: One resembles a pancake turner, but it has a shorter handle and a longer blade, about 8 inches long by 4 inches wide. The other is similar in size but, with the flick of a button, it fans out from one blade to three. The extra-wide surface is especially useful for lifting heavy pies.

the oven/

In Naples the typical pizza oven is dome-shaped and lined with fireproof bricks. When the oven is heated and a pizza is slid onto the oven floor or hearth, the heat from the hearth is immediately transferred to the dough. It springs up and becomes crusty and light.

To simulate this effect at home, you will need to line your oven with unglazed clay tiles or a baking stone. We prefer unglazed tiles because they are more durable. Baking stones sold in cookware shops for pizza and breadmaking are brittle and may crack after just a few uses at high temperatures. Supposedly, they harden with use, but ours have never lasted long enough to do so.

Another advantage of the tiles is that you can make the hearth as large as your oven can accommodate, while most baking stones are only 14 or 15 inches square or round. If you do buy a stone, buy a square or rectangular one rather than a round one for greater surface area.

At home, rinse the tiles under cool water. Never wash them with detergent, since they may pick up soapy flavors. Before using the tiles for baking, heat them in the oven first, then let them cool to season them. Place the tiles on a rack in the lower third of the oven. You do not have to remove a baking stone or tiles from the oven when you bake other foods. Don't worry about stains on the tiles, just scrape off any globs of food if necessary.

pizza cutter or pizza wheel/

Buy a sturdy pizza cutter with large cutting wheel, about 4 or 5 inches in diameter. Small ones are less effective in cutting through thick pies and crusty doughs.

When Michele worked in a magazine test kitchen, the pizza cutter of choice was a pair of kitchen shears. Aesthetically, shears are not as pleasing as a pizza wheel, but they do a very good job of making neat slices.

pizza peel/

A peel is a large paddle made of wood or metal, useful for sliding pizzas in and out of the hot oven. Peels are available in many cookware shops and catalogs (see page 201), or you can improvise one with a large rimless baking sheet. The dough tends to stick to the metal of the baking sheet, so flour it generously.

rolling pin/

While most pizza dough should be shaped and stretched by hand for maximum character, there are some instances when a rolling pin is needed to flatten the dough evenly and eliminate air pockets. The dough for piadina comes out very thin and flat without tearing, and stuffed pizzas have a more regular appearance if the dough is rolled out. Also, if you like a very thin, crackerlike pizza crust, use a rolling pin.

A rolling pin should be made of wood so that it will hold and stretch the dough. We like a heavy, straight French-style pin, but a ball bearing type is fine, too.

MARINARA con vongole
Aglio, Origano, Pomodoro e Prezzemolo
MARGHERITA
Pomodoro, Mozzarella, Formaggio e Basilico
MARGHERITA con uovo
Pomodoro, Mozzarella, Formaggio e Basilico
MARGHERITA con prosciutto
Pomodoro, Mozzarella, Formaggio e Basilico
MARGHERITA con funghi
Pomodoro, Mozzarella, Formaggio e Basilico
MARGHERITA alla romana
Mozzarella, Acciughe, Pomodoro e Basilico
MARGHERITA con prosciutto e funghi
Pomodoro, Mozzarella, Formaggio e Basilico
MARGHERITA con panna
Pomodoro, Mozzarella, Formaggio, Basilico e Panna
MARGHERITA con filetto pomodorini
Filetto di pomodoro, Fior di latte, Formaggio e Basilico
PIZZA al prosciutto crudo
Pomodoro, Mozzarella, Prosciutto crudo,
Formaggio e Basilico
PIZZA CAPRESE
Pomodoro per insalata, Mozzarella, Basilico ed Origano
PIZZA alla campagnola
Olive, Acciughe, Pomodoro, Capperi, Aglio ed Origano
PIZZA sostanziosa
Pomodoro, Mozzarella, Prosciutto, Uova,
Formaggio e Basilico
PIZZA lasagna
Pomodoro, Mozzarella, Ricotta, Prosciutto, Formaggio e
PIZZA forte
Salame piccante, Peperoni sottolio, Pomodoro,
Peperoncino e Basilico
PIZZA alle 4 stagioni

EL SANTA LUCIA
NAPOLI

how to make pizza dough

*t*here is nothing difficult about making pizza dough, but like winding spaghetti neatly on a fork or riding a two-wheeler, you need to understand the procedure and get the knack of how to do it. It may take a little practice, but once you have it, making pizza dough, or any kind of yeast dough, is a breeze.

Read these instructions carefully and envision the procedure before beginning. Make a small batch of dough the first time. Most importantly—do not invite twelve friends over for a pizza party until you are sure of your technique!

dissolving the yeast/

Pour the water into a 2-cup measure to allow room for stirring. The water temperature is important. Use warm tap water, or if you are using bottled water, heat it in a saucepan on top of the stove or in a cup in the microwave oven. The water should be warm to the touch—not hot or you may kill rather than activate the yeast cells. To make sure that the water temperature is correct, use an instant-reading thermometer. The temperature should be between 105° and 115°F. Yeast cells are light and tend to float and clump together when they are introduced to water. Sprinkle the yeast over the water and allow it to stand for a minute or so until it begins to soften. Stir the mixture with a spoon until all the clumps of yeast are dissolved.

measuring the flour/

Measure the flour by dipping a dry measuring cup into the flour container, then sweeping off the excess above the rim with a spatula or knife. Do not pack the flour down. Since flours differ in their ability to absorb liquid—depending on the area of the country, the weather, age and type of wheat, and many other factors—start with the lesser amount of flour given in the recipe, keeping the remainder handy to add if needed.

mixing the ingredients/

The dough can be mixed in a bowl with a wooden spoon. Simply combine the flour and any other dry ingredients with the salt in the bowl. Add the yeast mixture and other liquid ingredients and stir until the dough begins to form a rough ball.

When working with dough, Italians usually work without a bowl directly on a countertop or cutting board. Often, they use a special large wooden board, called a *spianatoia* or *tavolino,* which is reserved for dough and pasta. Since the board is never used for chopping onions or other smelly foods, it cannot transfer off flavors to the dough. Also, the wooden surface is just rough enough to grip the dough and help with the kneading. The board has a lip in front that stabilizes it against the table or countertop and a low wall in the back to help contain the ingredients. Some also have side walls. The flour is piled onto the board and a depression is made in the center. The Italians call this *fare la fontana,* or making a well. You can order a *tavolino* from *King Arthur's Baking Catalogue,* or you can use an ordinary wooden or rough plastic cutting board.

Charles makes pizza dough using the well method because he can better regulate the amount of flour and there is little cleanup involved afterward. No bowls or spoons are needed, just scrape the board with a dough scraper.

Pour the liquid ingredients into the center of the well. Stir the liquid, incorporating the flour little by little. Charles uses two fingers to stir with instead of a fork or spoon. He feels that it gives him better control and is less likely to break through the well of flour. If you try this method, stir gently and be very careful to keep

Use two fingers to stir the liquid into the flour for better control over the mixing.

Keep the outside of the flour wall high so that the liquid does not spill over the side.

Use a dough scraper to lift and turn the dough until it forms a ball.

the outside of the flour wall high, until enough flour from the inside of the crater has been incorporated so that the liquid is not runny. Things can get messy if the liquid overflows the flour. As the dough starts to form and hold a shape, use a dough scraper to help lift and turn it. Mix the dough just until a rough ball is formed. Some dry flour will remain on the board.

kneading the dough by hand/

At this point, the dough should be soft and rather sticky. A moist, sticky dough produces better pizza than a dry dough, so add as little of the extra flour as possible. Adding more flour makes the dough firm and easier to knead, but may also make it too dense and compact.

If you have made the dough directly on the board, set it aside for a moment. Scrape the board to remove any stuck-on particles of dough. Transfer the scrapings to a sieve to separate the flour from the hardened bits of dough. Shake the sieve to one side of the board. Discard the bits of dough left in the sieve.

Now you are ready to knead the dough. The purpose of kneading is to develop gluten, a stretchy protein that comes from working the flour and water together. Gluten gives the pizza dough structure and body.

Lightly dust the board or clean countertop with flour. A kneading surface with a bit of roughness or texture to it like wood is better than a glassy-smooth surface like marble or granite. If necessary, anchor the board by placing a damp paper towel underneath it so that it will not slide. Be sure your hands are clean and dry. Dust them lightly with flour.

Begin kneading by pushing the dough away from you with the heels of your hands, then pulling it back toward you with your fingertips. Repeat this motion, rotating the dough clockwise a quarter turn each time. Add flour a little at a time to

Knead by pushing the dough away from you with the heel of your hand and back toward you with your fingertips.

prevent the dough from sticking. Some professional bakers recommend using only one hand to knead, while keeping the other hand clean and free to use a dough scraper to lift and turn the dough.

Set a kitchen timer so you won't be tempted to stint on the kneading. The dough is ready when it looks smooth and satiny and feels moist, not dry and floury, which will take about 10 minutes by hand. If you pinch it and pull it out gently, it will have an elastic texture and slowly glide back to its original position. You should be able to pinch a piece of dough and stretch it slowly to four times its size without tearing.

making the dough by machine/

If you use a heavy-duty mixer, combine the dry ingredients with the paddle attachment, then add the liquid. Once the dough begins to come together, switch to the dough hook, adding just enough flour so that the dough forms a ball without sticking to the sides of the bowl. The mixer does a thorough job of kneading the dough in about 5 minutes.

A food processor does an excellent job of making dough, too. Use either the plastic kneading blade or the steel blade. The steel blade works better for small batches of dough because it is longer and reaches around the bowl and under the dough better than the shorter plastic blade. With larger batches of dough, the steel blade may cut through the dough and interfere with the gluten development.

If the blade sticks to the stem of your processor, try spraying the interior of the blade first with cooking spray before putting it in place. Add the dry ingredients and pulse to blend them. With the machine running, pour in the liquid. In a few moments, the dough will gather together into one or two balls and pull away from the bowl. If the dough is too soft, add flour a little at a time through the feed tube until the ball forms. The dough should be smooth and elastic in about 1 minute.

Pizza dough can also be mixed and kneaded in a bread machine. Follow the manufacturer's instructions.

When making pizza dough in a machine, we always knead it briefly by hand after removing it just to be sure that it feels right and to shape it.

rising the dough at room temperature/

To shape the dough into a ball, hold your hands out in front of you, palms up and fingers together. Place your hands to each side and under the ball. Tuck the

Place your upturned hands on each side and under the ball. Tuck the dough under, with the insides of your hands, stretching the outer surface smooth.

dough under, with the insides of your hands, stretching the outer surface smooth. Move your hands back and forth, rotating the ball clockwise.

The dough can rise on a countertop or in a bowl. If your kitchen is chilly, the bowl method is better, since you can place it in a cozy spot, such as a turned-off oven, in a cabinet, or on top of the refrigerator. Whichever method you use, the dough should not be exposed to air for any length of time or it will get crusty and difficult if not impossible to use.

To rise it on a countertop, place the dough seam side down. Cover the dough completely with a large overturned bowl or plastic wrap. Make sure to use a large enough bowl or sheet of plastic so that the dough remains covered as it expands. Weight the wrap down with kitchen utensils or other heavy objects.

To rise the dough in a bowl, brush it first with olive oil. Place the dough upside down in the bowl to oil the top, then turn the ball over so that the seam side is on the bottom. Cover the bowl with plastic wrap.

Leave the dough to rise at cool room temperature. The dough will begin to expand and rise as the yeast, activated by the warm water, feeds on the sugars in the flour. As it feeds, the yeast releases carbon dioxide, which becomes trapped in the stretchy bands of gluten. In 60 to 90 minutes, the dough will double in size. The longer and slower the rise, the more flavorful the dough.

rising the dough in the refrigerator/

Many pizza makers let their dough rise overnight in the refrigerator, since the cold temperature slows down the action of the yeast. This is also a convenient way to get the doughmaking step done ahead of time. Refrigerated dough keeps well for at least 24 hours.

To rise the dough in the refrigerator, pour a little olive oil into a large clean plastic bag. Close the bag and rub the sides together to coat the interior with oil. Place the dough in the bag, flattening the bag to remove air. If using a twist tie, seal the bag tightly near the opening. For a zipper-type bag, close it as you normally would. Place the bag in the refrigerator. After about an hour, flatten the dough and release the air from the bag. Repeat the flattening one or two more times. Once it is thoroughly chilled, the dough will rise more slowly. Place a heavy weight on top, such as a metal baking pan. For best results, use the dough within 24 hours.

For the second rise, make your hand into a fist and press the dough down to release the air. The dough may feel stickier now than before it rose, but do not add more flour at this point. Handle it as little as possible. With a knife, cut the dough into the number of pieces required in the recipe. Shape the pieces into balls, smoothing and rounding them as described on page 29. Place the balls on a lightly floured surface, leaving several inches between each. Cover the balls with plastic wrap and let the dough rise again. This should take about an hour.

If the dough has been refrigerated, the second rise will take 2 to 3 hours, depending on the temperature of the room. To speed up the rising time, the dough can be heated in a microwave oven.

Place the ball of a dough in a microwave-safe bowl. Cover with plastic wrap pierced with a few holes and put it in the microwave oven. Fill a 1-cup glass measure with water and put it in a far corner of the microwave. Microwave on defrost for 1 minute. Let rest for 5 minutes. Knead the dough briefly to warm it evenly. *Do not overheat the dough or it will cook instead of heat.* The dough will rise in about 1 hour.

shaping the dough by hand/

There are any number of ways to stretch the dough, but this is the one that many pizzaioli use. We like to stretch it by hand because the finished pizza has a natural look and texture, with bumps and blisters that enhance the taste.

Lightly flour your work surface. Keeping the remaining pieces covered, place 1 piece of dough on the surface, turning it over to flour the top. Holding your fingers flat, press the dough out into a disk. Continue to flatten the disk, pushing it out,

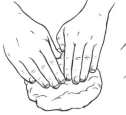
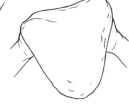

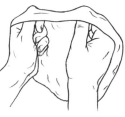

Holding your fingers flat, press the dough out into a disk.

Drape the circle of dough over your closed fists.

With your thumbs down, move your hands up and down, tugging and stretching the dough evenly.

Give the edge a final thinning by holding your thumbs up and stretching the dough between them.

thinning it, and making it larger. The border should remain slightly thicker than the center. Lift and turn the dough over from time to time. Handle it gently and work slowly to avoid tearing the dough. As it nears the desired dimensions, drape the circle of dough over your closed fists. Move your hands up and down tugging the dough and stretching it evenly. If the dough does tear, pinch it together to seal.

As an alternative method for the final thinning, hold the dough between your fingers and let the weight of the dough stretch it a little further.

shaping the dough with a rolling pin/

A rolling pin presses the air out of the dough evenly, eliminates air pockets, and makes a flatter, crisper, less chewy crust. This works well for double-crust pies, or if you like a wafer-thin crust, but for most flat pizzas a hand-shaped dough is the way to go.

To roll out the dough with a pin, place the ball on a lightly floured surface and flatten it into a disk with your fingers. Place the pin in the center of the disk and roll it away from you, stopping just as you reach the edge. Lift the pin and rotate the dough a quarter turn. Return the pin to the center of the dough. Repeat the rolling motion, rotating the disk after each turn. Do not roll the pin over the edge of the dough. If the dough sticks to the pin or the surface, dust it lightly with flour, but do not use any more flour than is necessary or the dough will become dried out.

baking/

At least 30 minutes to an hour before you plan to bake your pizzas, place the oven rack on the lowest level and arrange a stone or tiles on top. Heat the oven to the maximum temperature, 500° or 550°F.

Dust a pizza peel generously with flour. Once the dough reaches the desired size and shape, place it on the peel. Give the peel a shake or two to make sure that the pizza is not sticking. If it sticks, lift the dough and sprinkle the peel with more flour. Any that sticks to the bottom of the dough will become toasty and add flavor to the pie. Italians do not use cornmeal on the pizza peel. It changes the flavor and texture of the pizza, and we do not recommend it.

Do not leave the pizza dough sitting on the peel any longer than you have to or it may start to stick. Quickly spread the sauce, cheese, and other ingredients on the dough. Give the peel a shake every so often to make sure the dough is not sticking.

The order in which you add the toppings will affect the end result. Usually the sauce or tomatoes go on first, followed by the cheese, although some cheeses get rubbery when baked too long. To avoid this put the cheese on first, then the sauce or other ingredients. This way, the cheese is insulated from the other toppings. You can also bake the pie partway with just the sauce on it, then add the cheese in the last minute or two of cooking so that it melts. Spread the toppings to within ½ to ¾ inch of the edge of the pie to create a golden, crusty edge, or *cornicione*. Don't use toppings that are excessively wet or heavy or the dough will stick to the peel. When using a cooked topping, sauce, or filling for pizza, let it cool to room temperature so it will not steam and soften the dough.

When the toppings have been added, open the oven door and slide the peel into the oven. Place the front end of the peel at the back of the oven. Tilt the peel and jerk it gently so that the pizza begins to slide. When the dough touches the hot stone it will adhere. Gently slide the peel back, jerking it if necessary to keep the pizza moving. Once the pie is in the oven, quickly close the door and begin timing. In our ovens, a pie bakes in about 6 minutes, but the exact time may vary according to the type of stone or tiles you use and your oven.

If the pizza does not come off the peel as neatly as you would like or is misshapen, don't be too concerned. It will taste great anyway. Scrape any topping residue off the stone or peel with a metal spatula before making another pizza.

When the pie is browned and crisp around the edge, slide the peel or a large metal spatula under it. Transfer the pie to a cutting board and cut it into wedges with a pizza wheel.

Brandi®

La pizza... dal 1780

HOTEL SANTA LUCIA
NAPOLI

neapolitan pizza

*t*he experts agree: The world's finest pizza is made in Naples. Some say the air, the water, and the local ingredients make Neapolitan pizza special. That may be so, but we believe there is something else that makes a Neapolitan pie so excellent—the love and care given to its creation by the pizzaiolo, the pizza man.

Watching a Neapolitan pizza maker as he goes about his work is almost as enjoyable as eating the results. The pizza man moves swiftly and efficiently, flattening each ball of ivory-colored dough on his floury countertop and scattering slices of creamy mozzarella and crushed ripe tomatoes over the surface. After swirling a thin stream of olive oil over the pie, he deftly slides the disk onto his battered peel, jerking it once or twice to be sure that it will not stick, then tips it into the white-hot wood-fired oven. With the peel, he shuffles around the pizzas already in the oven to ensure even browning. He briefly turns away to ready two or three more pies, then sensing that the time is right, he removes the pizzas from the oven and slides them onto plates. A few leaves of sweet basil flutter to the surface and, perhaps, a dribble of fragrant olive oil. The whole process from shaping to topping to finished pizza takes less than 5 minutes.

In Italy the pizza man trains for his profession for many years, but his love for pizza and pride in his task is innate. Fortunately, you do not have to live in Naples to make or eat great pizza. All you need is enthusiasm and some pizza know-how.

When making Neapolitan-style pizzas at home, we shape them as they do in Naples, 9 to 10 inches in diameter. Italians serve these pizzas on dinner plates and eat them with knives and forks. Most home ovens, however, can only bake one pizza of this size at a time, so rather than serve it as an individual portion, cut the pie into wedges and share it.

neapolitan-style pizza dough

makes enough for four 9- to 10-inch pizzas

*i*n Naples the classic pizza measures about 9 to 10 inches and has a crust that is neither too thin nor too thick. The texture of the pie is soft and chewy. Neapolitans say the true test of a well-made pizza is whether it can be folded in half and then folded again, into quarters, without cracking or breaking the crust. Only the edge, called the cornicione, is crisp, though it too is chewy.

In Italy flour is softer than American flour because it is low in gluten, the protein that makes pizza dough and other baked goods chewy. Soft flour is great for making cakes and pastry, but not so good for pizza, so Italians blend their soft flour with hard American or Canadian flour, which they call "Manitoba." This flour, which is higher in gluten, gives Italian pizza dough the desired chewiness.

On this side of the Atlantic, we need to soften our flour to make an authentic Neapolitan-style dough, so we combine cake flour with all-purpose flour. This tender dough stretches easily and has less of a tendency to spring back on itself, so it is easier to shape. Neapolitan dough is made with less yeast, so it rises a bit more slowly—perfect for a long, slow overnight refrigerator rise, or a more rapid rise at room temperature. The longer rising time makes a slightly better-tasting crust, too.

> **1 teaspoon active dry yeast**
> **1¼ cups warm water (105° to 115°F)**
> **1 cup cake flour (not self-rising)**
> **2½ to 3 cups all-purpose flour**
> **2 teaspoons salt**
> **Olive oil for the bowl**

1. Sprinkle the yeast over the water. Let stand 1 minute, or until the yeast is creamy. Stir until the yeast dissolves.

2. In a large bowl, combine the cake flour, 2¹/₂ cups of the all-purpose flour, and the salt. Add the yeast mixture and stir until a soft dough forms. Turn the dough out onto a lightly floured surface and knead, adding more flour if necessary, until smooth and elastic, about 10 minutes.

3. Lightly coat a large bowl with oil. Place the dough in the bowl, turning it to oil the top. Cover with plastic wrap. Place in a warm, draft-free place and let rise until doubled in bulk, about 1¹/₂ hours.

4. Flatten the dough with your fist. Cut the dough into 2 to 4 pieces and shape the pieces into balls. Dust the tops with flour.

5. Place the balls on a floured surface and cover each with plastic wrap, allowing room for the dough to expand. Let rise 60 to 90 minutes, or until doubled.

6. Thirty to sixty minutes before baking the pizzas, place a baking stone or unglazed quarry tiles on a rack in the lowest level of the oven. Turn on the oven to the maximum temperature, 500° or 550°F.

7. Shape and bake the pizzas as described in the following recipes.

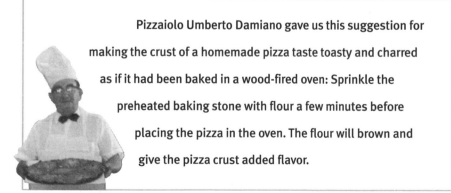

Pizzaiolo Umberto Damiano gave us this suggestion for making the crust of a homemade pizza taste toasty and charred as if it had been baked in a wood-fired oven: Sprinkle the preheated baking stone with flour a few minutes before placing the pizza in the oven. The flour will brown and give the pizza crust added flavor.

simple pizza sauce

SALSA SEMPLICE / *makes about 2½ cups*

*P*eople are amazed when we tell them that Neapolitans do not put tomato sauce on pizza, but it's true. Since commercial pizza ovens are so hot, a precooked sauce would burn and overcook while the pizza bakes. Instead, the typical tomato topping is nothing more than ripe, fresh crushed tomatoes or canned San Marzano tomatoes.

We find that while drained fresh, ripe tomatoes taste great, canned tomatoes cooked on a pizza in our home oven, no matter how good their quality, taste like canned tomatoes. The baking temperature in a home oven is not high enough so the tomatoes simply don't cook enough to become sweet. To counteract this, we simmer canned tomatoes briefly first with some oil and salt.

If you prefer a smooth sauce or use anything other than canned San Marzano tomatoes, puree the tomatoes first by passing them through a food mill. Do not use a food processor, which only grinds up the seeds and makes the sauce bitter.

> **1 can (28 ounces) Italian peeled tomatoes, preferably**
> **San Marzano, with their juice**
> **4 tablespoons olive oil**
> **Salt**

1. In a large saucepan, combine the tomatoes, oil, and salt to taste. Bring to a simmer.

2. Cook, stirring occasionally, until thickened, 15 to 20 minutes. Let the sauce cool before spreading it on the pizza dough.

variation: When vine-ripened tomatoes are at their peak in our area, we use them instead of canned and freeze a big batch of pizza sauce. Prepare the tomatoes as in step 1 of Summertime Fresh Tomato Sauce on page 39. Then follow the preceding instructions. Refrigerate the sauce up to 1 week or freeze it in 1- to 2-cup–size containers up to 3 months.

summertime
fresh tomato sauce—uncooked

makes about 2¹/₂ cups

*i*n Naples cherry tomatoes are very meaty with few seeds and little juice. When the tomatoes are very ripe, pizza makers crush them with their hands to make a simple uncooked sauce for pizza. We make the same type of sauce in the summer months using sweet, locally grown tomatoes. Do not use tasteless "hard ripe slicing tomatoes" when making this sauce.

> **2 large tomatoes or 6 plum tomatoes**
> **3 tablespoons olive oil**
> **1 tablespoon chopped fresh basil**
> **or ¹/₂ teaspoon dried oregano**
> **Salt and freshly ground black pepper**

1. Bring a medium saucepan of water to boiling. Add the tomatoes and leave them in the pan for 30 seconds. Remove the tomatoes with a slotted spoon. Cool them under running water. Cut the tomatoes in half through the core and cut away the stem ends. The skins should slip off easily. Squeeze the tomatoes to extract the juice and seeds. Chop the tomatoes coarsely.

2. In a bowl combine the tomatoes and the remaining ingredients. Let stand 30 minutes. Do not refrigerate.

pizza marinara

makes 1 pizza

*d*a Michele is one of the oldest and most famous pizzerias in Naples. Since it is located on a small street, we could not locate it on a street map, so we gave our hotel concierge the address and asked for directions. The concierge, a very haughty gentleman, took a look at the address and his eyebrows shot up. "I would not go there," he sniffed, implying that it was not in a safe or classy neighborhood. We went anyway and found the place surrounded by late-model Mercedes and BMWs and the entrance crammed with well-to-do Italians dressed in designer clothes. Hardly a threat by anyone's standards. The pizzeria was so crowded that we could not get in, so we returned the next day for an early lunch.

Simplicity is what makes Da Michele so special. The walls are white, simply decorated with a few poems and quotations about pizza. The menu is as basic as could be: Only pizza marinara and pizza margherita are served. No other toppings are available, no other kinds of pies are served, no appetizers, side dishes, or desserts. Ever. When you are that focused, you have to be good, and Da Michele's pizzas are some of the best we have eaten. Light and tender, they seem to melt in your mouth.

The pizzaiolo, a fellow whose uniform was as white as the walls, looked as if he had been casually turning out perfect pies all his life. When they saw us taking his picture, his assistants who work the oven demanded we take their photo, too.

Prepared dough for one 9-inch pizza

About ¹/₂ cup Simple Pizza Sauce (page 38), at room temperature

1 garlic clove, thinly sliced

Pinch of dried oregano

About 1 tablespoon olive oil

1. Place the dough on a floured surface. Holding your hands flat, pat the ball out evenly with your fingers, lifting it and turning it over several times, until it reaches a 9-inch circle. Do not handle the dough any more than is necessary. If the dough seems sticky, dust it lightly with flour.

2. Dust a pizza peel or a rimless cookie sheet with flour. Carefully transfer the circle of dough to the peel. Shake the peel once or twice to make sure the dough does not stick. If it does, sprinkle the peel with more flour.

3. Quickly top the dough with the sauce, spreading it to within ½ inch of the edge using the back of a spoon. Scatter the garlic and oregano over the sauce. Drizzle with the oil.

4. To slide the pizza onto the prepared baking stone, line up the edge of the peel with the back edge of the stone, then tilt the peel, jerking it gently to start the pizza moving. Once the edge of the pizza touches the stone, carefully pull back on the peel until the pizza is completely off. Once the pizza is on the stone, do not attempt to move it until it firms up in 2 or 3 minutes.

5. Bake 6 to 7 minutes, or until the dough is crisp and browned. Serve immediately.

Here are some pizza marinara variations we sampled elsewhere in Naples.

pizza alla romana / In step 3, in addition to the garlic and oregano, top the pizza with 4 to 6 drained anchovy fillets. In Rome this pizza is called alla Napoletana. In Naples, where all pizzas are alla Napoletana, this variation is called alla Romana.

old lady's face (Faccia Di Vecchia)/ In step 3 substitute thin slices of onion for the garlic. Sprinkle with toasted bread crumbs and grated pecorino Romano.

pizza inferno/ In step 3, after adding the garlic and oregano, sprinkle the pizza with capers, crushed red pepper, and grated pecorino Romano.

pizza forte/ In step 3, after adding the garlic and oregano, sprinkle the pizza with spicy pepperoni and drained hot pickled peppers.

pizza atomica / In step 3, after adding the garlic and oregano, sprinkle the pizza with crushed red pepper and black olives and layer with salami and mozzarella.

pizza mergellina / In step 3, eliminate the garlic. Top the pizza with one dozen steamed mussels, shells removed.

pizza all' ortolana (Kitchen-Garden Style)/ In step 3, eliminate the garlic. Top the sauce with peeled roasted red, green, and yellow bell peppers and a handful of pitted and sliced green olives.

pizza alla siracusana (Syracuse Style)/ In step 3, eliminate the garlic. Top the sauce with fried eggplant slices, mozzarella, oregano, roasted bell peppers, and green olives.

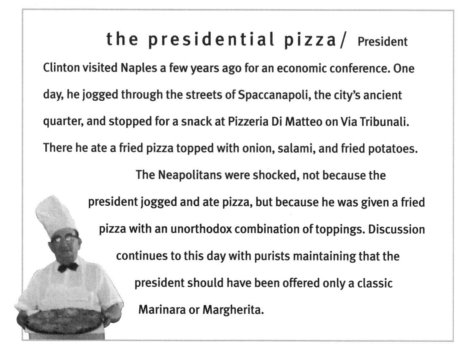

the presidential pizza/ President

Clinton visited Naples a few years ago for an economic conference. One day, he jogged through the streets of Spaccanapoli, the city's ancient quarter, and stopped for a snack at Pizzeria Di Matteo on Via Tribunali. There he ate a fried pizza topped with onion, salami, and fried potatoes.

The Neapolitans were shocked, not because the president jogged and ate pizza, but because he was given a fried pizza with an unorthodox combination of toppings. Discussion continues to this day with purists maintaining that the president should have been offered only a classic Marinara or Margherita.

pagnotiello

PIZZA POCKETS / *makes 1 pizza*

a *pagnotiello* looks more like a hot stuffed pita sandwich than a pizza, but it is made with pizza dough and served at Da Ettore, one of the finest pizzerias in Naples. The fresh mozzarella, prosciutto, and arugula stuffing is one of our favorites, but don't hesitate to invent your own combinations, like grilled vegetables and Fontina, roasted bell peppers and provolone, or salami and mozzarella.

Prepared dough for one 9-inch pizza
Sliced fresh mozzarella, sliced prosciutto, and
fresh arugula

1. Using a rolling pin, roll out the dough on a lightly floured surface to an 8- to 9-inch circle, turning it over once or twice. With a fork, pierce the dough all over the top.

2. Dust a pizza peel or the back of a baking sheet with flour. Place the dough on the peel, shaking it once or twice to make sure it does not stick. If it does, lift the dough and dust the peel or baking sheet with more flour.

3. Slide the dough into the oven and bake until the dough is puffed and lightly browned, about 4 minutes. Remove from the oven and place on a cutting board. Protect one hand with an oven mitt while you cut the pizza in half crosswise with a serrated knife, forming two pockets. Stuff the two halves with the cheese and prosciutto. Slide the pagnotiello back into the oven for 1 minute more, or until the cheese is softened.

4. Remove the pizza from the oven and stuff with the arugula. Serve hot.

pizza margherita

makes 1 pizza

*M*argherita was only seventeen when she became the wife of King Umberto I of Savoy, known as *il re buono,* the good king. After their marriage, Margherita and her new husband traveled around Italy. The people were delighted with the young queen, not just because of her beauty but also because she had the common touch and mingled with them, wearing the local peasant woman's headdress in Genoa and riding in a gondola in Venice, something that royalty usually did not do. Best of all, when the queen arrived in Naples, her new home, Vesuvius stopped erupting! Needless to say, the people loved her.

Tired of the fancy French fare served at court, the queen one day in 1889 asked if she could try some of the food that the common people ate. The best pizzaiolo in town was summoned. His name was Raffaele Esposito, and he was the owner of a pizzeria known as *Pietro e basta così,* meaning Pietro and that's enough. Raffaele brought along his wife, Pasqualina Brandi, as his assistant. The pair felt that it would be inappropriate to serve the queen the traditional pizza marinara with tomatoes, oregano, garlic, and oil, because garlic was just too common a food for a queen. Instead, the couple decided to prepare three types of pizza, all popular at that time—a white pizza with oil, cheese, and basil; one with *cecenielle,* tiny baby fish; and one with tomato, mozzarella, and basil.

Many versions of this story say that Raffaele actually invented this last pizza for the queen. This idea seems supported by the fact that the red, white, and green of the tomatoes, mozzarella, and basil are the colors of the Italian flag, so the pie could be regarded as a patriotic gesture. However, this is not true. Records dating to forty years before the queen's tasting indicate that pizza with mozzarella, tomato, and basil was eaten in Naples long before she tried it. At any rate, Queen Margherita loved

Esposito's three pizzas, especially the mozzarella version, so Raffaele named the pizza in her honor.

Raffaele's pizzeria still exists, though now it is called Pizzeria Brandi. On the wall is proudly displayed the letter dated June 11, 1889, that he received from the Royal House declaring his pizzas *buonissime*—the best!

Prepared dough for one 9-inch pizza
About ¹/₂ cup Simple Pizza Sauce (page 38), at room
   temperature
4 ounces mozzarella (use fresh mozzarella if possible),
   thinly sliced and torn into smaller pieces
1 tablespoon olive oil
3 to 4 large fresh basil leaves, torn into pieces

1. Place the dough on a floured surface. Holding your hands flat, pat the ball out evenly with your fingers, lifting it and turning it over several times, until it reaches a 9-inch circle. Do not handle the dough any more than is necessary. If the dough seems sticky, dust it lightly with flour.

2. Dust a pizza peel or a rimless cookie sheet with flour. Carefully transfer the circle of dough to the peel. Shake the peel once or twice to make sure the dough does not stick. If it does, sprinkle the peel with more flour.

3. Spread the tomato sauce on the dough, leaving a ¹/₂-inch border. Arrange the mozzarella slices on top. Drizzle with the oil.

4. To slide the pizza onto the prepared baking stone, line up the edge of the peel with the back edge of the stone, then tilt the peel, jerking it gently to start the pizza moving. When the edge of the pizza touches the stone, carefully pull back on the peel until the pizza is completely off. Once the pizza is on the stone, do not attempt to move it until it firms up in 2 or 3 minutes.

5. Bake 6 to 7 minutes, or until the dough is crisp and browned. Scatter the basil over the pizza. Serve immediately.

Pizza margherita has many variations in Italy. Here are just a few:

with cream (Margherita con Panna)/ Instead of oil, drizzle the pizza margherita with 2 tablespoons heavy cream.

with mushrooms and prosciutto (Margherita con Funghi e Prosciutto)/ Before baking, scatter 1 or 2 thinly sliced mushrooms over the pizza. After it is baked, top with thin slices of prosciutto.

with grated cheese/ Before baking, sprinkle the pizza with freshly grated pecorino Romano or Parmigiano-Reggiano.

bull's eye pizza (Pizza Occhio di Bue)/ Slide the pizza margherita into the oven. Break a raw egg into a cup and pour it onto the center of the pizza.

vesuvio/ Before baking, top the pizza margherita with anchovies, olives, capers, and crushed red pepper.

alla caprese/ Substitute Summertime Fresh Tomato Sauce (page 39) for Simple Pizza Sauce.

the ten commandments of pizza /

A few years back, members of the Naples Pizza Association came to the United States to lay down the laws of pizza making Neapolitan style. Here are the rules as published in the *New York Times*.

1. The dough must contain only flour, water, yeast, and salt. No fat is permitted.

2. Dough must be kneaded by hand or with approved mixers.

3. Dough must be punched down by hand, never mechanically or with a rolling pin.

4. The diameter of the pizza must never exceed 30 centimeters (about 12 inches).

5. The pizza must be baked directly on the floor of the oven, never on a pan.

6. The oven must be made of brick or similar material like volcanic stone. The fuel must be wood.

7. The oven temperature must be at least 400°C (750° to 800°F).

8. Marinara, a classic topping, must be made with tomato, oregano, garlic, olive oil, and salt; Margherita must be made with tomato, mozzarella, olive oil, basil, and salt.

9. The pizza must not be crusty but must be well done and fragrant with a high soft edge.

10. Variations on the classics can be inspired by tradition and fantasy, provided they are not in conflict with the rules of good taste and culinary laws.

prosciutto and arugula pizza

makes 1 pizza

*W*alking through Spaccanapoli, the old quarter in the heart of Naples, can be very difficult, as people and cars crawl slowly through the narrowest of streets to reach their destinations. We joined the throngs of students, shoppers, and deliverymen at lunchtime one bright February day on our way to Lombardi, one of the city's great pizzerias. Down the street, we could see the restaurant's sign, and we headed toward it against the tide of people, feeling like salmon swimming upstream.

At last we reached the pizzeria. Inside, we walked past the pizza oven, climbed a narrow winding staircase to the upper floor, and found a table in the corner. The service was brusque, but the pizzas were divine, especially the margherita topped with silken prosciutto and *rughetta,* a crisper, greener variation of the arugula that is grown here. This is one of our favorite pies.

> **Prepared dough for one 9-inch pizza**
> **About ½ cup Simple Pizza Sauce (page 38), at room**
>   **temperature**
> **2 ounces fresh mozzarella, thinly sliced**
> **1 cup arugula, tough stems removed**
> **3 to 4 very thin slices prosciutto**

1. Place the dough on a floured surface. Holding your hands flat, pat the ball out evenly with your fingers, lifting it and turning it over several times, until it reaches a 9-inch circle. Do not handle the dough any more than is necessary. If the dough seems sticky, dust it lightly with flour.

2. Dust a pizza peel or a rimless cookie sheet with flour. Carefully transfer the circle of dough to the peel. Shake the peel once or twice to make sure the dough does not stick. If it does, sprinkle the peel with more flour.

3. Spread the tomato sauce on the dough, leaving a $\frac{1}{2}$-inch border. Arrange the mozzarella slices on top.

4. To slide the pizza onto the prepared baking stone, line up the edge of the peel with the back edge of the stone, then tilt the peel, jerking it gently to start the pizza moving. Once the edge of the pizza touches the stone, carefully pull back on the peel until the pizza is completely off. When the pizza is on the stone, do not attempt to move it until it firms up in 2 or 3 minutes.

5. Bake 6 to 7 minutes, or until the dough is crisp and browned. Remove the pizza from the oven. Arrange the arugula over the cheese. Place the prosciutto on top. Serve immediately.

four seasons pizza

PIZZA QUATTRO STAGIONE / *makes 1 pizza*

*t*he name of this pizza refers to the four sections into which it is divided, each with its own separate topping. It's perfect for people who like variety—or for those who can't make up their minds! We put provolone, olives, sausage, and roasted peppers on ours, but you can substitute other toppings, such as marinated artichoke hearts, sautéed mushrooms, pepperoni, salami, or sliced onions. Some versions of this pizza have you make a divider between each section with strips of dough, but we prefer ours without.

Prepared dough for one 9-inch pizza
About ¹/₂ cup Simple Pizza Sauce (page 38), at room
  temperature
¹/₂ cup roasted, peeled red bell peppers
1 ounce provolone, mozzarella, or Fontina cheese, sliced
6 to 8 black olives, pitted and sliced
1 Italian sausage, cooked and sliced
1 tablespoon olive oil

1. Place the dough on a floured surface. Holding your hands flat, pat the ball out evenly with your fingers, lifting it and turning it over several times, until it reaches a 9-inch circle. Do not handle the dough any more than is necessary. If the dough seems sticky, dust it lightly with flour.

2. Dust a pizza peel or a rimless cookie sheet with flour. Carefully transfer the circle of dough to the peel. Shake the peel once or twice to make sure the dough does not stick. If it does, sprinkle the peel with more flour.

3. Spread the tomato sauce on the dough, leaving a ¹/₂-inch border. Place the roasted peppers, cheese, olives, and sausage on the dough, dividing them into 4 wedges. Drizzle with the olive oil.

4. To slide the pizza onto the prepared baking stone, line up the edge of the peel with the back edge of the stone, then tilt the peel, jerking it gently to start the pizza moving. When the edge of the pizza touches the stone, carefully pull back on the peel until the pizza is completely off. Once the pizza is on the stone, do not attempt to move it until it firms up in 2 or 3 minutes.

5. Bake 6 to 7 minutes, or until the dough is crisp and browned. Serve immediately.

the origins of pizza/

When we began working on this book, we were surprised to be told by a number of people that pizza is an American creation, brought to Italy and popularized there by the G.I.'s during World War II. We do not know how this nonsense became so widespread, but it is no more true than that old story about Marco Polo introducing pasta to Italy.

Pizza in one form or another is a very ancient food. The ancient Egyptians knew how to use yeast to make bread, as well as beer. The Etruscans ground wheat and other grains, mixed the meal with water and shaped it into flat cakes. The Greeks, who founded Naples and called it Partenope, baked flat loaves of bread seasoned with herbs and oil.

The origin of the word *pizza* is unclear, but some scholars believe that it is derived from Picentia, the name of a town near Naples. Flat bread began to be known as *picea,* and eventually pizza.

The earliest pizzas were probably simply seasoned with lard, garlic, and herbs. Later, little fish and grated cheese were used. Tomatoes, which were not native to the European continent, did not come into common usage in Italy until the nineteenth century.

pizza with garlic and oil

PIZZA AGLIO OLIO / *makes 1 pizza*

*g*arlic and oil are one of the oldest toppings for pizza. In the latter part of the eighteenth century, Emmanuele Rocca wrote in *Usi e Costumi di Napoli,* a book about Neapolitan customs, "The most ordinary pizza, called *coll'aglio e l'oglio* (with garlic and oil) has for its seasoning oil, and on top they spread, besides the salt, oregano and finely chopped cloves of garlic. Others are covered with grated cheese and moistened with lard, and on top there are placed a few leaves of basil. To the first tiny fish are often added; to the second thin slices of mozzarella. Some use sliced prosciutto, tomato, clams, etc. Some fold the dough over on itself in a form which they call *calzone*."

Prepared dough for one 9-inch pizza
3 large garlic cloves, chopped
2 tablespoons olive oil
$^1/_2$ teaspoon dried oregano
Pinch of crushed red pepper
Coarse or kosher salt

1. Place the dough on a floured surface. Holding your hands flat, pat the ball out evenly with your fingers, lifting it and turning it over several times, until it reaches a 9-inch circle. Do not handle the dough any more than is necessary. If the dough seems sticky, dust it lightly with flour.

2. Dust a pizza peel or a rimless cookie sheet with flour. Carefully transfer the circle of dough to the peel. Shake the peel once or twice to make sure the dough does not stick. If it does, sprinkle the peel with more flour.

3. Combine the garlic, oil, oregano, red pepper, and salt to taste. Spread the mixture over the dough.

4. To slide the pizza onto the prepared baking stone, line up the edge of the peel with the back edge of the stone, then tilt the peel, jerking it gently to start the pizza moving. Once the edge of the pizza touches the stone, carefully pull back on the peel until the pizza is completely off. Once the pizza is on the stone, do not attempt to move it until it firms up in 2 or 3 minutes.

5. Bake 6 to 7 minutes, or until the dough is crisp and browned. Serve immediately.

pizza calabrese/ Just before baking, top the pizza with slices of fresh mozzarella.

anchovy pizza / Top the pizza with pieces of drained anchovies.

moon pizza (della Luna)/ Brush the pizza dough with oil and nothing else. Bake the dough, flattening it once or twice with a metal spatula, until crisp and browned. Remove from the oven and spread with ¼ cup pesto sauce.

florentine pizza

PIZZA FIORENTINA / *makes 1 pizza*

*f*oods containing spinach are always dubbed alla Fiorentina, though no one seems to know why. Anyway, a combination of creamy ricotta, spinach, and onion makes a lovely pizza topping.

1/2 **pound fresh spinach**
1/4 **cup finely chopped onion**
1 **tablespoon olive oil**
1/2 **cup ricotta**
1/2 **cup freshly grated Parmigiano-Reggiano**
Salt and freshly ground black pepper
Prepared dough for one 9-inch pizza

1. Wash the spinach well in several changes of cool water. Remove the tough stems. Place the spinach in a large pot. Cover and steam in just the water that clings to the leaves until tender and wilted, about 5 minutes. Let cool. Drain the spinach and place it in a kitchen towel. Squeeze to extract the spinach juices. Finely chop the spinach.

2. In a small skillet, cook the onion in the oil over medium-low heat until tender but not browned, about 5 minutes.

3. In a bowl, combine the spinach, onion, ricotta, Parmigiano, and salt and pepper to taste.

4. Place the dough on a floured surface. Holding your hands flat, pat the ball out evenly with your fingers, lifting it and turning it over several times, until it reaches a 9-inch circle. Do not handle the dough any more than is necessary. If the dough seems sticky, dust it lightly with flour.

5. Dust a pizza peel or a rimless cookie sheet with flour. Carefully transfer the circle of

dough to the peel. Shake the peel once or twice to make sure the dough does not stick. If it does, sprinkle the peel with more flour.

6. Spread the spinach mixture over the dough, leaving a $^{1}/_{2}$-inch border. Immediately slide the pizza onto the baking stone, lining up the edge of the peel with the back edge of the stone, tilting the peel, and jerking it gently to start the pizza moving.

7. Bake 6 to 7 minutes, or until the edges are puffed and the crust is crisp and golden brown. Serve immediately.

the political pizza/ The Northern League

is a group of Italian politicians who advocate separating the upper regions of Italy from the lower. Their plan is to form a new state called Padania, named after the Po River, which traverses northern Italy from west to east. At one time, the movement was strong, but lately its supporters have dwindled. The turning point might have come when some of the more militant members began calling for a boycott of pizza. To the members of the Northern League, pizza is a symbol of southern Italy, which they accuse of being backward and lazy.

Most Italians greeted the suggestion of a pizza boycott with amusement. Even the leader of the Northern League, Umberto Bossi, had to disagree. "Pizza is irreplaceable," he stated. "If it didn't exist, it would have to be invented." To prove his moderate stance, Bossi and a group of his followers ate pizzas topped with spinach and asparagus, green being the official color of the Northern League.

popeye's pizza

PIZZA BRACCIA DI FERRO / *makes 1 pizza*

*P*opeye's name in Italian means literally "Iron Arms," which is synonymous with arm wrestling. Since Popeye the sailor man is a notorious spinach eater, he even has a pizza named in his honor. No doubt he would approve of the zesty gorgonzola or other blue cheese, garlic, and creamy pine nuts that complement the greens.

> **1 garlic clove, minced**
> **1 tablespoon olive oil**
> **$1/2$ pound fresh spinach, rinsed and stemmed**
> **Salt**
> **Prepared dough for one 9-inch pizza**
> **$1/4$ cup crumbled Gorgonzola or other blue cheese**
> **1 tablespoon pine nuts**

1. In a medium saucepan, cook the garlic in the oil over medium heat until golden, about 1 minute. Add the spinach and salt. Pour in a little water if the spinach is dry. Cover and cook 5 minutes, or until the spinach is wilted.

2. Pour the spinach into a strainer and press with the back of a spoon until the spinach mixture is quite dry. Chop the spinach coarsely.

3. Place the dough on a floured surface. Holding your hands flat, pat the ball out evenly with your fingers, lifting it and turning it over several times, until it reaches a 9-inch circle. Do not handle the dough any more than is necessary. If the dough seems sticky, dust it lightly with flour.

4. Dust a pizza peel or a rimless cookie sheet with flour. Carefully transfer the circle of dough to the peel. Shake the peel once or twice to make sure the dough does not stick. If it does, sprinkle the peel with more flour.

5. Quickly spread the spinach over the dough, leaving a ½-inch border. Sprinkle with the Gorgonzola and pine nuts.

6. To slide the pizza onto the prepared baking stone, line up the edge of the peel with the back edge of the stone, then tilt the peel, jerking it gently to start the pizza moving. When the edge of the pizza touches the stone, carefully pull back on the peel until the pizza is completely off. Once the pizza is on the stone, do not attempt to move it until it firms up in 2 or 3 minutes.

7. Bake 6 to 7 minutes, or until the dough is crisp and browned. Serve immediately.

Ciro Verde says: "To prevent mozzarella cheese from becoming tough and rubbery in a home oven, which bakes pizza more slowly than a professional oven, cover the disk of dough with tomato sauce and bake it partway before adding the cheese and other toppings. Slide the pizza under the broiler for a quick browning and the cheese will be perfectly melted."

Italians view with scorn American pizzas with their universal tomato sauce and innumerable toppings. One pizzaiolo said that this urge to go a good thing one better was "like putting arms on the Venus di Milo."

JOHN THORNE
Pizza: The Art of the Pizzaiolo

four cheese pizza

PIZZA QUATTRO FORMAGGI / *makes 1 pizza*

*W*hen Michele visited the Citro Dairy, outside Naples, she watched the cheesemakers smoking freshly made water buffalo mozzarella. The cheeses were suspended from a pole set over a big metal barrel where a smoky wood fire was burning. The cheesemakers prefer to use hickory and chestnut wood for the best flavor. A heavy piece of canvas was placed on top of the barrel, and the cheeses were left to absorb the smoke for a short time, just long enough for them to turn from creamy white to a light coffee color, but not to melt from the heat.

Smoked mozzarella is delicious in sandwiches or as a pizza topping—or served as an antipasto along with roasted bell peppers. It is available here, but make sure to look for mozzarella that has been smoked over wood, not dipped in an artificially flavored smoke solution.

Prepared dough for one 9-inch pizza
2 ounces fresh goat cheese
1 ounce Gorgonzola, crumbled
2 thin slices fresh mozzarella
2 thin slices smoked mozzarella
Olive oil for drizzling

1. Place the dough on a floured surface. Holding your hands flat, pat the ball out evenly with your fingers, lifting it and turning it over several times, until it reaches a 9-inch circle. Do not handle the dough any more than is necessary. If the dough seems sticky, dust it lightly with flour.

2. Dust a pizza peel or a rimless cookie sheet with flour. Carefully transfer the circle of dough to the peel. Shake the peel once or twice to make sure the dough does not stick. If it does, sprinkle the peel with more flour.

3. Quickly scatter the goat cheese and Gorgonzola on top of the dough, and arrange the mozzarella slices over all. Drizzle with the oil.

4. To slide the pizza onto the prepared baking stone, line up the edge of the peel with the back edge of the stone, then tilt the peel, jerking it gently to start the pizza moving. Once the edge of the pizza touches the stone, carefully pull back on the peel until the pizza is completely off. Once the pizza is on the stone, do not attempt to move it until it firms up in 2 or 3 minutes.

5. Bake 6 to 7 minutes, or until the dough is crisp and browned. Serve immediately.

> Yet just try and make it anywhere other than Naples. Just try and mix the flour with water that is not from the Serino, or have the dough flattened by anyone other than a pizzaiolo, one of the heirs to a tradition that goes back into the recesses of time. Just try to make it without local olive oil or lard, or tomatoes that have not ripened between the Sebeto and the Sele, or crown it with basilico that hasn't grown under the sun of Naples; try to place it in the oven without that certain lilting, rhythmic step. As for the oven, it must be as large as a room, ardent as the blood that flows through the veins of a young girl, and burning bundles of the very driest vine branches that barely leave ashes. Without all of this, what kind of pizza could you ever hope to obtain?
>
> **MARIO STEFANILE**
> *Naples Guide,* **Naples Chamber of Commerce**

eggplant parmesan pizza

makes 2 pizzas

*S*ometimes eggplant skin can be very tough, but if it is removed, the eggplant loses its shape. Our solution is to partially peel off the skin, giving the slices a pretty striped edge.

1 medium eggplant

3 tablespoons olive oil

4 medium tomatoes

1 garlic clove, finely chopped

2 tablespoons shredded fresh basil

Salt and freshly ground black pepper

4 ounces thinly sliced mozzarella (fresh if possible)

Prepared dough for two 9-inch pizzas

2 tablespoons freshly grated Parmigiano-Reggiano

1. Preheat the oven to 450°F. Oil a large baking sheet.

2. With a swivel blade vegetable peeler, remove lengthwise strips of the eggplant skin, about 1 inch apart. Cut the eggplant into thin slices crosswise and arrange them on the baking sheet. Brush the slices with 2 tablespoons of the oil. Bake 10 minutes, or until the eggplant is browned and tender. With a metal spatula, remove the eggplant from the baking sheet and let cool.

3. Raise the oven heat to the maximum, 500° to 550°F.

4. Cut the tomatoes in half and squeeze them gently to eliminate the seeds and excess liquid. Chop the tomatoes and combine them with the remaining oil, the garlic, basil, salt and pepper to taste.

5. Place 1 ball of the dough on a floured surface. Holding your hands flat, pat the ball out evenly with your fingers, lifting it and turning it over several times, until it reaches a 9-inch circle. Do not handle the dough any more than is necessary. If the dough seems sticky, dust it lightly with flour.

6. Dust a pizza peel or a rimless cookie sheet with flour. Carefully transfer the circle of dough to the peel. Shake the peel once or twice to make sure the dough does not stick. If it does, sprinkle the peel with more flour.

7. Quickly spoon half the tomato mixture over the dough. Arrange half the eggplant slices on top and sprinkle with half the mozzarella and Parmigiano.

8. To slide the pizza onto the prepared baking stone, line up the edge of the peel with the back edge of the stone, then tilt the peel, jerking it gently to start the pizza moving. Once the edge of the pizza touches the stone, carefully pull back on the peel until the pizza is completely off. Once the pizza is on the stone, do not attempt to move it until it firms up in 2 or 3 minutes.

9. Bake 6 to 7 minutes, or until the dough is crisp and browned. Serve immediately.

10. Make a second pizza with the remaining ingredients.

> The Neapolitans have claimed pizza as their own invention to which they have a passionate attachment. To them it is much more than a simple food; it is a cult that brings a gleam to their eyes, a celebratory rite of the joy that they take in living.
>
> ELIZABETH ROMER
> *Italian Pizza and Hearth Breads*

pizza american style

*A*mericans eat more than a billion tons of pizza each year—or more than one hundred million slices a month, or seventy-five acres of pizza a day! Classic toppings like cheese, sausage, and pepperoni are the most popular choices, but it is only natural that new varieties of pizza have evolved and taken on an American accent. Some are close to their Italian roots in that they use local ingredients to great effect, such as pizza with sun-dried tomatoes and goat cheese. Others, like the Thai barbecued chicken pizza with coconut which we once spotted on a menu, are a little too far afield to be a part of this collection of Italian-style pizzas.

The good news is that American pizzas are good and getting better all the time, and not just in cities with Italian enclaves like New York, where a wave of new pizzerias has opened in the past few years. These include La Pizza Fresca, Polistina's, Naples 45, Patsy Grimaldi's in Brooklyn and several others. In Washington, D.C., we like Pizzeria Paradiso. Believe it or not, our favorite American pizzeria is in Phoenix, Arizona, where a talented young pizzaiolo by the name of Chris Bianco has been making pizza for several years. A Bronx native, Chris learned his craft in Naples. Chris says the secret is simple: Use only the finest ingredients, like organic flour, perfect tomatoes, and handmade fresh mozzarella. Whenever we taste Chris's pizza, we are sorry that there isn't a Pizzeria Bianco near us.

Here, then, is a collection of some of our favorite Italian American-style pizzas that we have sampled around the country.

basic dough for two 12-inch pizzas

*t*his dough differs from the Neapolitan-style dough on (page 36) in that it yields a crisper, chewier pie than the other. If you prefer, this quantity of dough can be shaped into four 9-inch pizzas.

1 envelope active dry yeast (2^1/$_4$ teaspoons)
1^1/$_3$ cups warm water (105° to 115°F)
3^1/$_2$ to 4 cups unbleached all-purpose flour
2 teaspoons salt
Olive oil for the bowl

1. Sprinkle the yeast over the water. Let stand 1 minute, or until the yeast is creamy. Stir until the yeast dissolves.

2. In a large bowl, combine the 3^1/$_2$ cups flour and the salt. Add the yeast mixture and stir until a soft dough forms. Turn the dough out onto a lightly floured surface and knead, adding more flour if necessary, until smooth and elastic, about 10 minutes.

3. Lightly coat a large bowl with oil. Place the dough in the bowl, turning it to oil the top. Cover with plastic wrap. Place in a warm, draft-free place and let rise until doubled in bulk, about 1^1/$_2$ hours.

4. Flatten the dough with your fist. Cut the dough into 2 pieces and shape the pieces into balls. Flatten the dough slightly. Dust the tops with flour. Place the balls of dough on a floured surface and cover each with plastic wrap, allowing room for the dough to expand. Let rise 60 minutes, or until doubled.

5. Thirty to sixty minutes before baking the pizzas, place a baking stone or unglazed quarry tiles on a rack in the lowest level of the oven. Turn on the oven to the maximum temperature, 500° or 550°F.

6. Shape and bake the pizzas as described in the following recipes.

dough for one 12-inch pizza or two 9-inch pizzas

1 teaspoon active dry yeast

²/₃ cup warm water (105° to 115°F)

2 cups unbleached all-purpose flour

1 teaspoon salt

Olive oil for the bowl

Follow the instructions for Basic Dough (page 64) for two 12-inch pizzas.

> The pizza is really just an irregular shaped 200-gram ball of dough which has been left to rise. It's important to get the right moment to start rolling it out on the floured marble, beat it and then knead it so as to produce a circular pancake about the same shape as the Bay of Naples—thin and almost transparent in the middle, and as rugged as its coastline around the edges. Easier said than done; in effect it is like taming a wild beast—just try getting it ready to receive the bits of mozzarella, like white sails, the tomatoes, like the sails of the Turk, and the green basil leaves which bear all similarity to the crests of dark waves.
>
> **DOMENICO REA**
> *Naples Guide*, Naples Chamber of Commerce

how to eat pizza / What is the correct way to eat pizza, with your hands or with a knife and fork? We say it depends on the place and the pie.

In this country most pizza is served cut into wedges. The crust is firm yet pliable enough to bend in half and enclose the toppings. This minimizes sloppiness and the pizza can be eaten out of hand, which is perfectly acceptable. If you prefer, you can leave the slice flat on your plate and cut it with a knife and fork, but as you get toward the crisper, thicker part of the crust, the crust tends to be firmer and harder to cut. The pizza becomes cold as you saw away, so it is probably a better idea to pick up the balance of the slice and eat it with your hands.

In Italy, pizza in restaurants is served as a whole, individual-size pie. The crust is softer and the filling wetter than most pizzas served here, so pizza eaters cut theirs into small pieces and eat them with a fork. Some cut their pie into small wedges and eat them out of hand. If it is a street pizza, one purchased to be eaten as you walk instead of in a restaurant, the pie is smaller and has fewer and drier toppings. This type of pizza is folded into quarters and called *al portafoglio*—like a wallet, and eaten out of hand, wrapped in a piece of paper.

How you eat your pizza is up to you, but the deciding factor should be the consistency of the pie. If it is soft in the center and the toppings are wet, it is definitely a fork-and-knife pie. Firmer pies with drier or fewer toppings can be eaten with your hands.

the pizza maker's sauce

SALSA PIZZAIOLA / *makes about 3 cups*

*i*n Naples this spicy sauce is called alla pizzaiola, pizza maker's style, because it uses ingredients a pizzaiolo would have on hand—tomatoes, garlic, olive oil, oregano, and *peperoncini*, tiny fiery dried red chiles. Usually served as a sauce for thin beefsteaks, it is also good over spaghetti and, of course, pizza. This is the kind of sauce most pizzerias in this country use.

> **2 large garlic cloves, finely chopped**
> **Pinch of crushed red pepper**
> **3 tablespoons olive oil**
> **1 can (28 ounces) crushed tomatoes**
> **1 teaspoon dried oregano**
> **Salt**

1. In a large skillet, cook the garlic and red pepper in the oil over medium heat until the garlic is golden, about 1 minute. Add the tomatoes, oregano, and salt to taste. Bring to a simmer.

2. Cook, stirring occasionally, until thickened, or 10 to 15 minutes. Let the sauce cool before spreading it on the pizza dough. This sauce keeps well in the refrigerator for up to 5 days or in the freezer for 1 month.

pizza alla vodka

makes 2 pizzas

*g*oodfella's Brick-Oven Pizza of Staten Island and Brooklyn, New York, is famous for their spicy pizza with tomato, cream, and vodka sauce. This rich and tasty pie, inspired by a famous '80s pasta dish, has won several prizes in an annual contest sponsored by *Pizza & Pasta* magazine, an industry publication. Here is a home version of this award-winning pizza.

SAUCE

1 tablespoon butter

1 large garlic clove, finely chopped

¼ cup vodka

1 cup peeled fresh or canned tomatoes, chopped

Crushed red pepper

Salt

½ cup heavy or whipping cream

¼ cup fresh or frozen peas

Prepared dough for two 12-inch pizzas

4 ounces sliced mozzarella

½ cup thinly sliced mushrooms (3 to 4)

2 tablespoons grated pecorino Romano

1 tablespoon chopped fresh basil

2 tablespoons chopped prosciutto

1. To make the sauce, melt the butter in a medium saucepan over medium heat. Add the garlic and cook 30 seconds, or until lightly golden. Add the vodka and cook about 1 minute more until the alcohol evaporates.

2. Add the tomatoes, red pepper, and salt to taste. Simmer 10 minutes.

3. Add the cream and peas. Cook until the sauce is reduced and thickened, about 5 minutes more. Let cool.

4. Place 1 ball of the dough on a floured surface. Holding your hands flat, pat the ball out evenly with your fingers, lifting it and turning it over several times, until it reaches a 12-inch circle. Do not knead the dough or handle it any more than is necessary. If the dough seems sticky, dust it lightly with flour.

5. Dust a pizza peel or a rimless cookie sheet with flour. Carefully transfer the circle of dough to the peel, reshaping it as needed. Shake the peel once or twice to make sure the dough does not stick. If it does, sprinkle the peel with more flour. Quickly top the dough with the sauce, spreading it to within $1/2$ inch of the edge with the back of a spoon. Layer with half the mozzarella, mushrooms, and a sprinkling of pecorino.

6. To slide the pizza onto the prepared baking stone, line up the edge of the peel with the back edge of the stone, then tilt the peel, jerking it gently to start the pizza moving. Once the edge of the pizza touches the stone, carefully pull back on the peel until the pizza is completely off. After the pizza is on the stone, do not attempt to move it until it firms up in 2 or 3 minutes.

7. Bake the pizza 6 to 7 minutes, or until the cheese is melted and the crust is browned. Just before serving, sprinkle with half of the prosciutto and basil ingredients.

peperoni pepperoni pizza

makes 2 pizzas

*P*eperoni is the Italian word for bell peppers, while *pepperoni* is the American word for spicy dried sausage. What a difference a *p* makes! Peperoni with pepperoni makes a delicious pizza topping.

> **4 large bell peppers (about 2 pounds)**
> **2 medium onions**
> **2 tablespoons olive oil**
> **1 teaspoon dried oregano**
> **Pinch of crushed red pepper**
> **2 cups canned tomatoes with their juice, chopped**
> **Salt**
> **Prepared dough for two 12-inch pizzas**
> **4 ounces thin-sliced pepperoni**
> **2 tablespoons freshly grated pecorino Romano or**
>   **Parmigiano-Reggiano cheese**

1. In a large skillet, combine the peppers, onions, oil, oregano, red pepper, and $1/3$ cup water. Cover and cook, stirring occasionally, until the vegetables are crisp tender, about 15 minutes. If the vegetables begin to stick, add a little more water. Add the tomatoes and cook until most of the liquid has evaporated and the peppers and onions are tender. Add salt to taste. Let cool.

2. With your hands, flatten 1 ball of the dough out on a lightly floured surface. Handling it gently and turning it frequently, pat it into a 12-inch circle. Dust a pizza peel or baking sheet with more flour. Arrange the dough on the peel, reshaping the dough as needed. Shake the peel once or twice to be sure that the dough is not sticking. If it is, lift it carefully and dust the bottom with more flour.

3. Working quickly, spoon half the pepper mixture over the dough. Arrange half the pepperoni on top and sprinkle with half of the cheese.

4. Place the front edge of the peel on the edge of the baking stone farthest from you, jerk it gently to get the pizza moving, then slide the pizza onto the stone.

5. Bake 6 to 7 minutes, or until the pizza crust is golden brown and crisp. Slide the peel under the pizza and transfer it to a cutting board. Cut the pizza into slices.

6. Make a second pizza with the remaining ingredients.

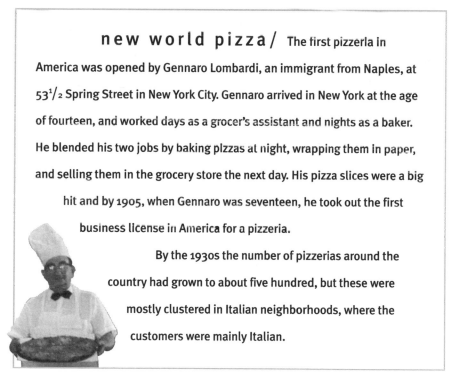

n e w w o r l d p i z z a / The first pizzeria in America was opened by Gennaro Lombardi, an immigrant from Naples, at 53$^1/_2$ Spring Street in New York City. Gennaro arrived in New York at the age of fourteen, and worked days as a grocer's assistant and nights as a baker. He blended his two jobs by baking pizzas at night, wrapping them in paper, and selling them in the grocery store the next day. His pizza slices were a big hit and by 1905, when Gennaro was seventeen, he took out the first business license in America for a pizzeria.

By the 1930s the number of pizzerias around the country had grown to about five hundred, but these were mostly clustered in Italian neighborhoods, where the customers were mainly Italian.

new haven–style garlic and cheese pizza bianca

makes 1 pizza

*i*n 1925, a young man named Frank Pepe began selling pizza in New Haven's Little Italy neighborhood from the back of a horsedrawn wagon. Eventually, the young baker opened a pizzeria on Wooster Street and named it Frank Pepe's Pizzeria Napoletana. Relatives and former employees opened pizzerias nearby and thus began a tradition for great pizza in Connecticut.

Frank Pepe's restaurant is still there, and the pizzas are baked in the same enormous coal-fired oven that has been lit almost constantly for more than sixty years. It is shut down only for a short time each fall, when the pizzeria closes for vacation.

The enormous, chewy pies are works of art—irregularly shaped, blistered, and charred—everything great pizza should be. The restaurant is still owned by members of Frank Pepe's family, who proudly make pies just the same way Frank did.

Prepared dough for one 12-inch pizza
1¹/₂ tablespoons olive oil
1 large garlic clove, finely chopped
¹/₂ teaspoon dried oregano
2 ounces thinly sliced mozzarella, torn into smaller pieces
2 ounces thinly sliced Fontina
1 tablespoon grated pecorino Romano

1. Place the dough on a floured surface. Holding your hands flat, pat the ball out evenly with your fingers, lifting it and turning it over several times, until it reaches 12 inches in diameter. Do not knead the dough or handle it any more than is necessary. If the dough seems sticky, dust it lightly with flour.

2. Dust a pizza peel or a rimless cookie sheet with flour. Carefully transfer the circle of dough to the peel, reshaping it as needed. Shake the peel once or twice to make sure the dough does not stick. If it does, sprinkle the peel with more flour.

3. Combine the oil, garlic, and oregano. Arrange the mozzarella and Fontina slices over the dough and sprinkle with the pecorino. Scatter the oil-garlic-oregano mixture over the cheese and drizzle with more oil.

4. To slide the pizza onto the prepared baking stone, line up the edge of the peel with the back edge of the stone, then tilt the peel, jerking it gently to start the pizza moving. Once the edge of the pizza touches the stone, carefully pull back on the peel until the pizza is completely off. After the pizza is on the stone, do not attempt to move it until it firms up in 2 or 3 minutes.

5. Bake the pizza 6 to 7 minutes, or until the cheese is melted and the crust is browned. Remove the pizza to a cutting board. Cut into wedges and serve.

variation Before adding the cheese, scatter cooked broccoli florets or spinach over the dough.

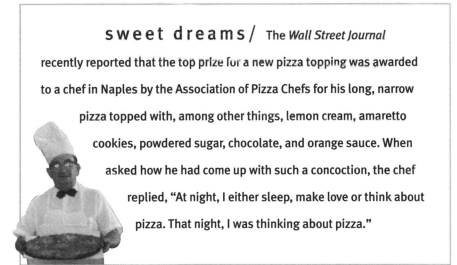

sweet dreams / The *Wall Street Journal* recently reported that the top prize for a new pizza topping was awarded to a chef in Naples by the Association of Pizza Chefs for his long, narrow pizza topped with, among other things, lemon cream, amaretto cookies, powdered sugar, chocolate, and orange sauce. When asked how he had come up with such a concoction, the chef replied, "At night, I either sleep, make love or think about pizza. That night, I was thinking about pizza."

white clam pizza

makes 1 pizza

*O*n busy days pizza lovers line up for hours to get a taste of this deliciously simple pie at The Spot in New Haven, Connecticut. A waiter circulates through the crowd assembled in the parking lot, taking pizza orders from hungry patrons long before they will be allowed inside.

Only fresh clams are used to make this pizza and the restaurant runs out of them early. One of the saddest sights is the NO CLAMS sign posted in the window, though most diners are easily consoled with a slice of pizza bianca.

1 pound small clams, such as Manila clams
4 garlic cloves, thinly sliced
Pinch of crushed red pepper
2 tablespoons olive oil
2 tablespoons chopped fresh parsley
Prepared dough for one 12-inch pizza
1 tablespoon freshly grated pecorino Romano

1. Soak the clams in cold water for about 30 minutes. Scrub the shells with a brush. Place the clams in a large saucepan with 2 tablespoons water. Cover and steam 4 to 5 minutes, shaking the pot occasionally, until the clams begin to open. Remove the open clams, leaving those that remain closed on the heat a little longer. If any clams refuse to open, discard them.

2. Drain the clam juice into a small bowl. Remove the meat from the shells. If they are sandy, rinse the clams one at a time in the clam juice. Strain the juice through a damp paper towel set over a sieve.

3. In a medium saucepan, cook the garlic and the red pepper in the oil over medium heat until the garlic is golden. Add the clam juice and bring it to a simmer. Cook until the juice is reduced to 1 or 2 tablespoons.

4. Remove the saucepan from the heat. Stir in the clams and parsley.

5. Place a pizza stone or tiles on the lowest level of the oven. At least 30 minutes to an hour before making the pizza, preheat the oven to 500° or 550°F.

6. Place the dough on a floured surface. Holding your hands flat, pat the ball out evenly with your fingers, lifting it and turning it over several times, until it reaches a 12-inch circle. Do not knead the dough or handle it any more than is necessary. If the dough seems sticky, dust it lightly with flour.

7. Dust a pizza peel or a rimless cookie sheet with flour. Carefully transfer the circle of dough to the peel, reshaping it as needed. Shake the peel once or twice to make sure the dough does not stick. If it does, sprinkle the peel with more flour.

8. With a slotted spoon, remove the clams from the sauce and scatter them over the dough. Drizzle the dough with 1 tablespoon of the sauce. Sprinkle with the cheese.

9. To slide the pizza onto the prepared baking stone, line up the edge of the peel with the back edge of the stone, then tilt the peel, jerking it gently to start the pizza moving. Once the edge of the pizza touches the stone, carefully pull back on the peel until the pizza is completely off. After the pizza is on the stone, do not attempt to move it until it firms up in 2 or 3 minutes.

10. Bake the pizza 6 to 7 minutes, or until the edges are puffed and the crust is crisp and golden brown. Remove the pizza to a cutting board. Drizzle with more sauce. Cut into wedges and serve immediately.

sonoma dried tomato pizza

makes 1 pizza

*e*very year we receive a gift of a fresh batch of dried tomatoes from Ruthie Waltenspiel, owner of California's Sonoma Foods. The tomatoes are dry yet full of concentrated tomato flavor—perfect for soups, sauces, and, of course, on top of pizza. Here we combine them with other favorite components of California cuisine, garlic and goat cheese, to make this pizza. Twelve garlic cloves may seem like a lot, but gently simmering them in olive oil tames the flavor and turns the garlic mellow. Save the leftover garlic oil to add to a salad dressing.

> ¹⁄₄ **cup olive oil**
>
> **12 garlic cloves, peeled**
>
> **Prepared dough for one 12-inch pizza**
>
> **6 to 8 marinated sun-dried tomatoes, drained and**
> **chopped (or use dried tomatoes soaked 10 minutes**
> **in warm water)**
>
> **1 teaspoon chopped fresh thyme leaves**
> **or ¹⁄₂ teaspoon dried thyme**
>
> **6 ounces fresh goat cheese, sliced**

1. In a small saucepan, combine the oil and garlic. Bring to a simmer over low heat. Cook 10 to 15 minutes until the garlic is lightly golden. Let cool. Drain the garlic, reserving the oil.

2. Place the dough on a floured surface. Holding your hands flat, pat the ball out evenly with your fingers, lifting it and turning it over several times, until it reaches a 12-inch circle. Do not knead the dough or handle it any more than is necessary. If the dough seems sticky, dust it lightly with flour.

3. Dust a pizza peel or a rimless cookie sheet with flour. Carefully transfer the circle of dough to the peel, reshaping it as needed. Shake the peel once or twice to make sure the dough does not stick. If it does, lift the dough and sprinkle the peel with more flour.

4. Brush the dough with some of the reserved garlic oil. Scatter the garlic cloves, chopped sun-dried tomatoes, and thyme over the dough. Arrange the slices of goat cheese on top. Drizzle with some more reserved garlic oil.

5. To slide the pizza onto the prepared baking stone, line up the edge of the peel with the back edge of the stone, then tilt the peel, jerking it gently to start the pizza moving. Once the edge of the pizza touches the stone, carefully pull back on the peel until the pizza is completely off. After the pizza is on the stone, do not attempt to move it until it firms up in 2 or 3 minutes.

6. Bake the pizza 6 to 7 minutes, or until the crust is browned. Cut into wedges and serve immediately.

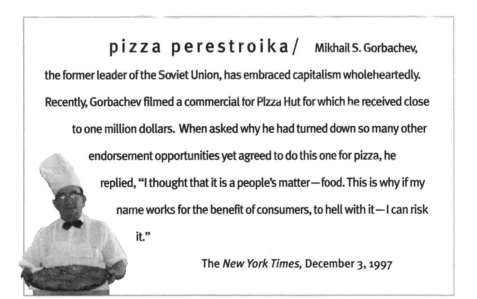

pizza perestroika/ Mikhail S. Gorbachev, the former leader of the Soviet Union, has embraced capitalism wholeheartedly. Recently, Gorbachev filmed a commercial for Pizza Hut for which he received close to one million dollars. When asked why he had turned down so many other endorsement opportunities yet agreed to do this one for pizza, he replied, "I thought that it is a people's matter—food. This is why if my name works for the benefit of consumers, to hell with it—I can risk it."

The *New York Times*, December 3, 1997

gorgonzola and onion pizzas

makes 2 pizzas

a few years ago, we visited the Napa Valley in California. At the suggestion of our friend Tony Di Dio, a pizza lover, great cook, and connoisseur of wine and food, we ate at Tra Vigne restaurant in St. Helena. There we had a marvelous pizza topped with sweet caramelized onions and creamy blue cheese. Here is our version of that heavenly pie. In keeping with its Napa Valley origins, we serve it with Zinfandel, a wine that goes well with hearty pizzas.

> **3 tablespoons olive oil**
>
> **2 medium onions, thinly sliced**
>
> **$1/4$ cup finely chopped sun-dried tomatoes**
>
> **1 garlic clove, finely chopped**
>
> **1 teaspoon chopped fresh thyme leaves**
>
>   **or $1/4$ teaspoon dried thyme**
>
> **Salt and freshly ground black pepper**
>
> **Prepared dough for two 12-inch pizzas**
>
> **$1/2$ cup crumbled Gorgonzola**
>
> **2 tablespoons freshly grated Parmigiano-Reggiano**

1. In a large skillet, cook the oil and the onions over low heat until golden, about 15 minutes. If the onions begin to brown too quickly, add a couple of tablespoons of water. Stir in the tomatoes, garlic, thyme, and salt and pepper to taste. Cook 1 minute more. Remove from the heat and let cool.

2. Place 1 ball of the dough on a floured surface. Holding your hands flat, pat the ball out evenly with your fingers, lifting it and turning it over several times, until it reaches a 12-inch circle. Do not knead the dough or handle it any more than is necessary. If the dough seems sticky, dust it lightly with flour.

3. Dust a pizza peel or a rimless cookie sheet with flour. Carefully transfer the circle of dough to the peel, reshaping it as needed. Shake the peel once or twice to make sure the dough does not stick. If it does, lift the dough and sprinkle the peel with more flour.

4. Quickly spread half the onion mixture over the dough with the back of a spoon to within 1/2 inch of the edge. Sprinkle with half of both cheeses.

5. To slide the pizza onto the prepared baking stone, line up the edge of the peel with the back edge of the stone, then tilt the peel, jerking it gently to start the pizza moving. Once the edge of the pizza touches the stone, carefully pull back on the peel until the pizza is completely off. After the pizza is on the stone, do not attempt to move it until it firms up in 2 or 3 minutes.

6. Bake the pizza 6 to 7 minutes, or until the crust is browned. Cut into wedges and serve immediately. Make a second pizza with the remaining ingredients.

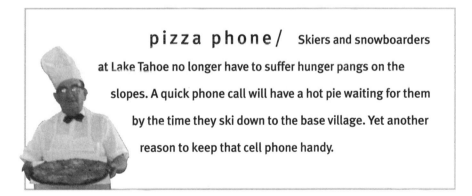

pizza phone/ Skiers and snowboarders at Lake Tahoe no longer have to suffer hunger pangs on the slopes. A quick phone call will have a hot pie waiting for them by the time they ski down to the base village. Yet another reason to keep that cell phone handy.

fig and taleggio pizza

makes 2 pizzas

*i*talians often serve cheese with honey, a brilliant combination. Charles adores figs and will eat them happily anytime, anywhere. When he saw this pizza combining honey, cheese, and figs on the menu at a restaurant in Cambridge, Massachusetts, he had to try it—and loved it!

Prepared dough for two 12-inch pizzas
2 tablespoons olive oil
1/2 cup ricotta
8 ounces Taleggio or Fontina, cut into 1/2-inch pieces
12 fresh sage leaves, torn into tiny pieces
4 to 6 ripe figs, cut into 1/4-inch slices
1/2 cup freshly grated Parmigiano-Reggiano
2 tablespoons honey

1. Place 1 ball of the dough on a lightly floured surface. Holding your hands flat, pat the ball out evenly with your fingers, lifting it and turning it over several times, until it reaches a 12-inch circle. Do not knead the dough or handle it any more than is necessary. If the dough seems sticky, dust it lightly with flour.

2. Dust a pizza peel or a rimless cookie sheet with flour. Carefully transfer the circle of dough to the peel. Shake the peel once or twice to make sure the dough does not stick. If it does, sprinkle the peel with more flour. Reshape the dough as needed to form a circle. Brush the dough with some of the oil. Spread with half the ricotta, leaving a 1/2-inch border all around. Sprinkle with half the Taleggio and sage. Arrange half the fig slices on top. Sprinkle with half the Parmigiano and drizzle with 1 tablespoon honey.

3. To slide the pizza onto the prepared baking stone, line up the edge of the peel with the back edge of the stone, then tilt the peel, jerking it gently to start the pizza moving. Once the edge of the pizza touches the stone, carefully pull back on the peel until the pizza is completely off. After the pizza is on the stone, do not attempt to move it until it firms up in 2 or 3 minutes.

4. Bake the pizza 6 to 7 minutes, or until the crust is browned. Cut into wedges and serve immediately. Make a second pizza with the remaining ingredients.

Take a tip from our friends at Seattle's Pagliacci Pizza: Vary pizza toppings to take advantage of seasonal and fresh local ingredients. This pizzeria's fall/winter menu includes specialty pizzas like Mushroom Primo, with a variety of mushrooms from the Pacific Northwest; Pear Primo, with fresh Washington State pears; and festive Spinaci Primo, with fresh tomatoes, cheese, and spinach arranged to look like a holiday wreath.

pizza alla don

makes 2 pizzas

*O*ur friend Don Pintabona is the chef at Tribeca Grill, a classic New York restaurant. He is also a serious pizza lover and went so far as to install in his Brooklyn backyard a small wood-burning pizza oven that he bought in Naples. We make up a few batches of our pizza dough and go there for a party. Don sets out an assortment of cheeses, meats, and vegetables, and everyone rolls up their sleeves and competes to make the best pizza. This recipe is a recent winning combination of Don's invention.

Red balsamic vinegar has been made in Italy for hundreds of years and became popular here about ten years ago. White balsamic vinegar is a modern invention not traditionally made in Italy. We love Don's idea of reducing the vinegar to a honey-like syrup. The syrup keeps well and you can serve it over strawberries or figs, or with cheese or salads.

> 1 cup white balsamic vinegar
>
> 1 tablespoon unsalted butter
>
> 1 large, firm, ripe pear, peeled, cored, and cut into 1/4-inch-thick slices
>
> Prepared dough for two 9-inch pizzas
>
> 1/2 cup crumbled Gorgonzola or other blue cheese
>
> 4 to 6 very thin slices prosciutto

1. Pour the vinegar into a small saucepan. Bring to a simmer over medium-low heat. Cook, swirling the pan occasionally, until the syrup is reduced and thickened and resembles honey, about 10 minutes. Let cool. (The syrup can be made ahead to this point. If it becomes too firm as it cools, simply reheat it with a few drops of water, or microwave it for 10 seconds.)

2. In a small skillet, heat the butter over medium heat. Add the pear slices and cook until tender, about 5 minutes.

3. Place 1 ball of the dough on a floured surface. Holding your hands flat, pat the ball out evenly with your fingers, lifting it and turning it over several times, until it reaches a 12-inch circle. Do not knead the dough or handle it any more than is necessary. If the dough seems sticky, dust it lightly with flour.

4. Dust a pizza peel or rimless cookie sheet with flour. Carefully transfer the circle of dough to the peel, reshaping it as needed. Shake the peel once or twice to make sure the dough does not stick. If it does, lift the dough and sprinkle the peel with more flour.

5. Arrange half the pears on the shaped dough. Scatter half the cheese on top. Drizzle with half the vinegar syrup.

6. To slide the pizza onto the prepared baking stone, line up the edge of the peel with the back edge of the stone, then tilt the peel, jerking it gently to start the pizza moving. Once the edge of the pizza touches the stone, carefully pull back on the peel until the pizza is completely off. After the pizza is on the stone, do not attempt to move it until it firms up in 2 or 3 minutes.

7. Bake the pizza 6 to 7 minutes, or until the crust is browned. Remove the pizza from the oven and arrange the prosciutto slices on top. Cut into wedges and serve immediately. Make a second pizza with the remaining ingredients.

tony d's pizza

makes 1 pizza

*i*n contrast to Don Pintabona's untraditional pear pizza, Tony Di Dio created this classic pizza with both fresh tomatoes and tomato sauce, though he could not resist adding a drizzle of balsamic vinegar to heighten the tomato flavor even more.

Prepared dough for one 12-inch pizza
¹/₂ cup Simple Pizza Sauce (page 38)
¹/₄ cup seeded chopped fresh tomato
1 teaspoon balsamic vinegar
2 or 3 slices smoked mozzarella, torn into 1-inch pieces
3 to 4 thin slices prosciutto, cut into thin strips

1. Place the dough on a lightly floured surface. Holding your hands flat, pat the ball out evenly with your fingers, lifting it and turning it over several times, until it reaches a 12-inch circle. Do not knead the dough or handle it any more than is necessary. If the dough seems sticky, dust it lightly with flour.

2. Dust a pizza peel or a rimless cookie sheet with flour. Carefully transfer the circle of dough to the peel, reshaping it as needed. Shake the peel once or twice to make sure the dough does not stick. If it does, lift the dough and sprinkle the peel with more flour.

3. Spread the tomato sauce on the dough. Scatter the tomatoes on top. Drizzle with the vinegar. Place the cheese on top.

4. To slide the pizza onto the prepared baking stone, line up the edge of the peel with the back edge of the stone, then tilt the peel, jerking it gently to start the pizza moving. Once the edge of the pizza touches the stone, carefully pull back on the peel until the pizza is completely off. After the pizza is on the stone, do not attempt to move it until it firms up in 2 or 3 minutes.

5. Bake the pizza 6 to 7 minutes, or until the crust is browned. Just before serving, top with the prosciutto. Cut into wedges and serve immediately.

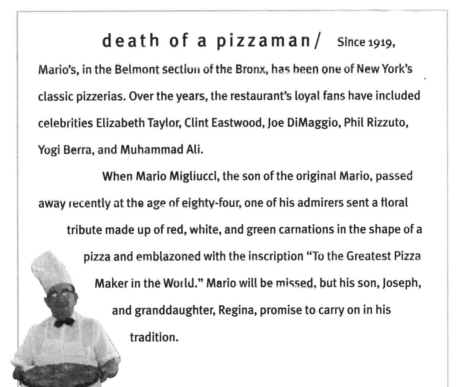

death of a pizzaman/ Since 1919,

Mario's, in the Belmont section of the Bronx, has been one of New York's classic pizzerias. Over the years, the restaurant's loyal fans have included celebrities Elizabeth Taylor, Clint Eastwood, Joe DiMaggio, Phil Rizzuto, Yogi Berra, and Muhammad Ali.

When Mario Migliucci, the son of the original Mario, passed away recently at the age of eighty-four, one of his admirers sent a floral tribute made up of red, white, and green carnations in the shape of a pizza and emblazoned with the inscription "To the Greatest Pizza Maker in the World." Mario will be missed, but his son, Joseph, and granddaughter, Regina, promise to carry on in his tradition.

grilled fresh tomato pizza
with three cheeses

PIZZA ALLA GRIGLIA / *makes 1 pizza*

*W*hen we first heard about grilling pizza, all we could think about was that the soft dough would slip through the grill and land on the hot coals, creating a terrible mess. But the idea of having fresh pizza without having to heat up the kitchen on a hot day was so appealing, we tried it. Now we make grilled pizzas all the time. Cooked on a grill, pizzas come out crisp and chewy with a delicious smoky accent.

You can adapt many pizza recipes to cooking on the grill, but avoid those with toppings that need to be fully cooked, such as seafood. The shaped dough is placed without topping on the hot grill. In a minute or so, grill marks appear and the dough firms up enough so that it can be moved or flipped over. Quickly cover the pizza with the toppings and grill until the crust is crisp and the toppings are heated through. Move the pizza around so that it cooks evenly without charring.

2 plum tomatoes, chopped

1 tablespoon chopped fresh parsley or basil

1 small garlic clove, minced

1 tablespoon olive oil

Salt and freshly ground black pepper

2 tablespoons grated Parmigiano-Reggiano

1/4 cup crumbled Gorgonzola

2 ounces fresh mozzarella, thinly sliced

Prepared dough for one 12-inch pizza

1. In a bowl, combine the tomatoes, parsley, garlic, oil, and salt and pepper to taste.

2. In another bowl, combine the cheeses.

3. Prepare a barbecue grill, using hardwood charcoal if possible. Set the grill rack about 4 inches from the coals.

4. Place the dough on a lightly floured surface. With your fingers, pat and stretch the dough out to a 12-inch circle.

5. Dust a pizza peel or the back of a baking sheet with flour. Place the dough on the peel, shaking it once or twice to be sure it does not stick. If it does, lift the dough and dust the peel or baking sheet with more flour.

6. Have the topping ingredients ready and at your side. Slide the dough onto the grill. In about 1 minute, the dough will stiffen and grill marks will appear on the bottom. If the coals are too hot, the dough may begin to char. Move it to a cooler spot on the grill.

7. When the dough is lightly browned and crisp, remove it to a cutting board and turn it cooked side up. Immediately add the tomato and cheese toppings. Slide the pizza back on the grill. Cook until the bottom crust is browned, the tomatoes are heated through, and the cheeses are melted, about 2 minutes more. To make sure that the cheese melts, especially on windy days, close the cover on the grill briefly or cover the pizza with a large pot lid or a tent made of aluminum foil. Serve hot.

robiola and truffle pizza

makes 1 pizza

*C*iro Verde of Da Ciro restaurant in New York makes great thin, crispy-crust pizzas. One Saturday at i Trulli restaurant Ciro gave us a pizzamaking lesson. He told us how he had learned to make pizza in Naples and gave us pointers on how best to use a wood-burning oven and how to improve our technique. A highlight of this session was Ciro's recipe for this tasty pie stuffed with robiola cheese and drizzled with truffle oil, which he claims to have invented.

First, the dough is flattened with a rolling pin to eliminate air pockets. Then the dough is pierced with a docker, an instrument that punctures the dough and helps to prevent it from puffing up too much in the oven. The flattened disk of dough is baked without any topping. When it is partially done, it is removed from the oven, split in half, and spread with cheese, then baked a second time until brown. Just before serving, the pie is drizzled with truffle oil. Since it is so rich, we like it best cut into wedges as an appetizer.

Robiola is a creamy cow's milk cheese. Soft fresh goat cheese is a good substitute. If you don't have truffle oil, which is available at many gourmet shops, the pizza will taste great anyway.

1 ounce robiola or fresh goat cheese without rind
Pinch of very finely chopped fresh garlic
Prepared dough for one 9-inch pizza
Truffle oil, optional

1. About 30 minutes before baking the pizza, preheat the oven to 500° or 550°F.

2. Place the cheese in a small bowl and add the garlic. (If using goat cheese, add a spoonful or two of cream or milk to make it spreadable.) Mash the cheese and garlic until blended.

PIZZA MARGHERITA, PAGE 44

PROSCIUTTO AND ARUGULA PIZZA, PAGE 48

PIZZA MARINARA, PAGE 40

PEPERONI PEPPERONI PIZZA, PAGE 70

SAUSAGE AND CHEESE DEEP-DISH PIZZA, PAGE 94

CAULIFLOWER AND BROCCOLI PIZZA, PAGE 120

POTATO, FENNEL, AND ONION CALZONI, PAGE 127

DORA'S PANZEROTTI, PAGE 132

PIADINA WITH MIXED GREENS AND GARLIC, PAGE 140

PIADINA WITH PROSCIUTTO, MORTADELLA, AND SALAMI, PAGE 138

PIADINA WITH NUTELLA, PAGE 138

GRILLED FOCACCIA WITH VEGETABLES AND ROBIOLA, PAGE 155

3. Using a rolling pin, roll out the dough on a lightly floured surface to an 8- to 9-inch circle. With a fork, pierce the dough all over the top. Dust a pizza peel or the back of a baking sheet with flour. Place the dough on the peel, shaking it once or twice to make sure it does not stick. If it does, lift the dough and dust the peel with more flour.

4. When the dough is browned underneath and slightly puffed, remove it from the oven and place it on a cutting board. Protect one hand with an oven mitt while you split the dough into 2 layers with a serrated knife. Remove the top layer and spread the bottom with the cheese mixture. Replace the top and press it lightly. Slide the pizza back into the oven for 2 minutes more, or until the top is lightly browned.

5. Remove the pizza from the oven and drizzle with truffle oil, if using. Cut and serve.

ciro's chocolate pizza

*A*ll of the Marzovillas grew up eating Nutella, a sweet chocolate hazelnut spread, that is the equivalent of peanut butter and jelly to an Italian child. Their mother, Dora, would spread it on bread for them for breakfast and for after-school snacks. One day Carmella and Domenica were having dinner at Da Ciro restaurant and discovered that the chef had come up with this variation on his famous robiola pie. The sisters were so excited that they called their brother Nicola to come to the restaurant to taste it. Despite the fact that his own restaurant i Trulli was packed with customers, Nicola could not resist the thought of a Nutella pizza. He put Charles in charge and rushed over to taste it. He says this pie transports him to his childhood in Apulia.

Prepared dough for one 9-inch pizza
About ½ cup Nutella (chocolate hazelnut spread)

Follow the instructions for the robiola pizza, substituting the Nutella for the cheese filling.

follonico's summer seafood pizza

makes 1 pizza

a wood-burning oven casts a warm and welcome glow on the dining room of New York's Follonico restaurant, named for a little town in Tuscany. In the evening the oven is used to cook all kinds of roasted meats, fish, and vegetables, but at lunchtime it bakes exceptional pizzas. The crust is thin, light, crisp, and slightly chewy with a bit of smoky flavor. We can't decide which pizza we like more—the one topped with lightly charred roasted vegetables or this seafood pizza, which Chef Alan Tardi says he serves only in the summer when fresh tomatoes are perfect.

> **6 small clams**
> **6 mussels**
> **4 small shrimps, peeled**
> **$\frac{1}{2}$ cup chopped fresh tomatoes**
> **1 tablespoon chopped fresh parsley**
> **Salt**
> **Prepared dough for one 12-inch pizza**
> **$\frac{1}{2}$ cup Simple Pizza Sauce (page 38)**
> **Olive oil**

1. Soak the clams and mussels in cold water for about 30 minutes. Scrub the shells with a brush. Place the shellfish in a large saucepan with 2 tablespoons water. Cover and steam 4 to 5 minutes, shaking the pot occasionally, until you hear a slight popping sound that indicates the shells are beginning to open. Remove the open clams and mussels, leaving any that remain closed on the heat about 1 minute more. If any refuse to open, discard them.

2. Drain the juice into a small bowl. Remove the meat from the shells. If they are sandy, rinse the clams and mussels one at a time in the juice. (The juices can be strained and frozen for use in seafood soups.)

3. Cut the shrimps in half lengthwise. Place them in a bowl with the mussels and clams, tomatoes, parsley, and salt to taste.

4. Place the dough on a floured surface. Holding your hands flat, pat the ball out evenly with your fingers, lifting it and turning it over several times, until it reaches a 12-inch circle. Do not knead the dough or handle it any more than is necessary. If the dough seems sticky, dust it lightly with flour.

5. Dust a pizza peel or a rimless cookie sheet with flour. Carefully transfer the circle of dough to the peel, reshaping it as needed. Shake the peel once or twice to make sure the dough does not stick. If it does, sprinkle the peel with more flour.

6. Spread the sauce over the dough, leaving a ½-inch border around the edge. Scatter the seafood mixture over the sauce. Drizzle with oil.

7. To slide the pizza onto the prepared baking stone, line up the edge of the peel with the back edge of the stone, then tilt the peel, jerking it gently to start the pizza moving. Once the edge of the pizza touches the stone, carefully pull back on the peel until the pizza is completely off. After the pizza is on the stone, do not attempt to move it until it firms up in 2 or 3 minutes.

8. Bake the pizza 6 to 7 minutes, or until the crust is browned and the shrimps are pink. Sprinkle with salt. Cut into wedges and serve immediately.

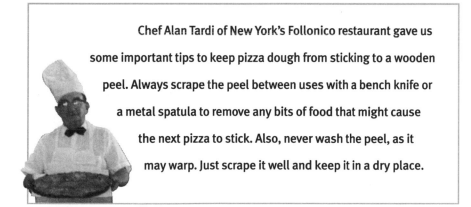

Chef Alan Tardi of New York's Follonico restaurant gave us some important tips to keep pizza dough from sticking to a wooden peel. Always scrape the peel between uses with a bench knife or a metal spatula to remove any bits of food that might cause the next pizza to stick. Also, never wash the peel, as it may warp. Just scrape it well and keep it in a dry place.

follonico's roasted vegetable pizza

makes 1 pizza

*O*ne of the most popular pizzas at Follonico restaurant in New York City is this one topped with roasted vegetables. You can add a sprinkling of grated cheese if you like, though it is fine without it. This is a perfect pizza for vegetarians.

Prepared dough for one 12-inch pizza
1 cup Simple Pizza Sauce (page 38) or Pizza Maker's
    Sauce (page 67)
1/2 recipe Roasted Vegetables (page 188)
1 tablespoon grated pecorino Romano, optional
Olive oil
Salt

1. Place the dough on a floured surface. Holding your hands flat, pat the ball out evenly with your fingers, lifting it and turning it over several times, until it reaches a 12-inch circle. Do not knead the dough or handle it any more than is necessary. If the dough seems sticky, dust it lightly with flour.

2. Dust a pizza peel or a rimless cookie sheet with flour. Carefully transfer the circle of dough to the peel, reshaping it as needed. Shake the peel once or twice to make sure the dough does not stick. If it does, lift the dough and sprinkle the peel with more flour.

3. Spread the sauce over the dough, leaving a 1/2-inch border around the edge. Arrange the vegetables on top. Sprinkle with the cheese, if using. Drizzle with the oil.

4. To slide the pizza onto the prepared baking stone, line up the edge of the peel with the back edge of the stone, then tilt the peel, jerking it gently to start the pizza moving. Once the edge of the pizza touches the stone, carefully pull back on the peel. After the pizza is on the stone, do not attempt to move it until it firms up in 2 or 3 minutes.

5. Bake the pizza 6 to 7 minutes, or until the crust is browned. Sprinkle with salt. Cut into wedges and serve immediately.

chicago deep-dish pizza dough

makes enough for two 9-inch deep-dish pizzas

*O*nce, Michele was returning from Chicago and was planning to take a flight that would arrive in New York in time for dinner. Knowing that the cupboard was bare at home, she made a quick stop at Chicago's famed Pizzeria Uno and bought one of their hefty frozen sausage and cheese pies. The airline personnel eyed the pizza box knowingly—and hungrily—and passed it through their metal detectors. A phone call home from somewhere over Philadelphia got the oven preheated and a bottle of wine ready. Not long after that we were enjoying our bubbling hot and savory souvenir from Chicago.

Chicago-style pizza is baked in a layer cake–type pan and smothered with toppings. This recipe makes enough dough for two pies with a moderately thick crust. Note that this dough rises only one time.

> 1 package active dry yeast
> 1 cup warm water (105° to 115°F)
> 2 tablespoons olive oil
> 3 to 3½ cups unbleached all-purpose flour
> ½ cup whole wheat flour
> 2 teaspoons salt

1. Sprinkle the yeast over the water. Stir until the yeast is dissolved. Stir in the oil.

2. In a large bowl, combine 3 cups of the all-purpose flour, the whole wheat flour, and the salt. Add the yeast mixture and stir until a soft dough forms. Knead 10 minutes, adding more flour if necessary, or until the dough is smooth and elastic.

3. Lightly oil a large bowl. Add the dough, turning it once to oil the top. Cover with plastic wrap and let rise in a warm place about 1 hour, or until doubled in bulk.

4. Divide the dough in half. Punch the dough down to eliminate air bubbles. Shape and bake the pizzas.

sausage and cheese deep-dish pizza

makes 2 deep-dish pizzas

*t*he sausage sauce in this recipe makes about 4 cups, enough for two hearty 9-inch deep-dish pizzas. If you only want to make one pizza, you can use the remaining sauce another day—it will keep in the refrigerator for at least three days—or you can freeze it. It also makes a fine pasta sauce.

SAUSAGE AND TOMATO SAUCE

1 tablespoon olive oil

**1 pound Italian sausage, skinned
and crumbled**

1 red bell pepper, chopped

2 large garlic cloves, finely chopped

$^1/_2$ teaspoon dried oregano

**1 can (28 ounces) Italian peeled tomatoes with their
juice, chopped**

Salt

Prepared dough for two 9-inch deep-dish pizzas

4 ounces thinly sliced provolone

4 ounces thinly sliced fresh mozzarella

1. In a large skillet, heat the oil over medium heat. Add the sausage and bell pepper, and cook, stirring frequently, until lightly browned.

2. Stir in the garlic and oregano, and cook 1 minute more.

3. Add the tomatoes. Bring to a simmer and add salt to taste. Cook until the sauce is very thick, about 1 hour. Let cool.

4. Preheat the oven to 400°F. Oil two 9 × 1½-inch layer cake pans.

5. With a rolling pin, roll out 1 ball of the dough to a 12-inch circle. Fit the dough into the prepared pan, patting it up the sides. Repeat with the remaining dough.

6. Spread 1 cup sauce in the pan. Top with half the provolone slices. Spread 1 more cup of sauce over the provolone. Arrange half the mozzarella slices on top. Make a second pizza with the remaining ingredients.

7. Bake 40 minutes, or until the crust is crisp and the filling is bubbling.

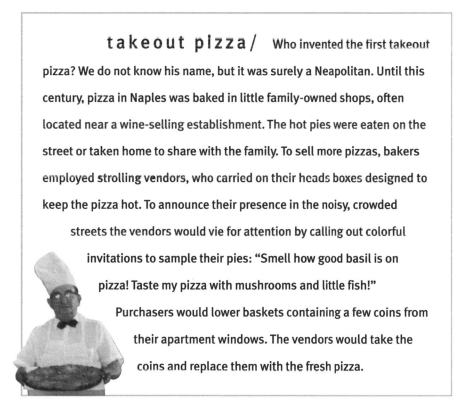

takeout pizza/ Who invented the first takeout pizza? We do not know his name, but it was surely a Neapolitan. Until this century, pizza in Naples was baked in little family-owned shops, often located near a wine-selling establishment. The hot pies were eaten on the street or taken home to share with the family. To sell more pizzas, bakers employed strolling vendors, who carried on their heads boxes designed to keep the pizza hot. To announce their presence in the noisy, crowded streets the vendors would vie for attention by calling out colorful invitations to sample their pies: "Smell how good basil is on pizza! Taste my pizza with mushrooms and little fish!" Purchasers would lower baskets containing a few coins from their apartment windows. The vendors would take the coins and replace them with the fresh pizza.

vegetable deep-dish pizza

makes 1 deep-dish pizza

*t*he citizens of Chicago have the reputation of being meat eaters, so we were surprised to find that deep-dish vegetable pizzas are popular there. With all the other good stuff in this hearty pie, you'll never miss the meat. It's a great way to get kids to eat their veggies. You can vary the filling according to whatever vegetables are in season. Just make sure to cook them first and drain them well or the vegetable juices will make the crust soggy.

1 pound fresh spinach

One 10-ounce package mushrooms

2 tablespoons olive oil

2 large garlic cloves, finely chopped

Salt and freshly ground black pepper

Prepared dough for one 9-inch deep-dish pizza

4 ounces sliced asiago or provolone

1 cup Pizza Maker's Sauce (page 67), at room temperature

4 ounces sliced fresh mozzarella

2 tablespoons grated pecorino Romano

1 tablespoon chopped fresh basil, optional

1. Wash the spinach well and discard the tough stems. Place the wet spinach in a large pot. Cover and bring to a simmer. Cook until the spinach is wilted and tender, about 5 minutes. Place the cooked spinach in a strainer and press it with a spoon to remove as much of the juice as possible. Chop the spinach on a board.

2. Wipe the mushrooms clean with a damp cloth and slice. In a large skillet, cook the mushrooms in the oil over medium heat until the liquid has evaporated and the mushrooms are beginning to brown. Add the garlic and cook 2 minutes more. Stir in the spinach and salt and pepper to taste. Mix well and remove from the heat. Let cool.

3. Preheat the oven to 400°F. Oil a 9 × 1½-inch layer cake pan or a deep-dish pie pan.

4. With a rolling pin, roll out the dough to a 13-inch circle. Arrange the dough in the prepared pan, patting it up the sides.

5. Place the slices of asiago in the bottom of the pan. Spread a layer of the vegetables over the cheese. Make a layer of sauce. Arrange the mozzarella slices on top. Sprinkle with the pecorino.

6. Bake until the crust is crisp and the filling is bubbling, about 40 minutes. Sprinkle with basil, if using, and serve.

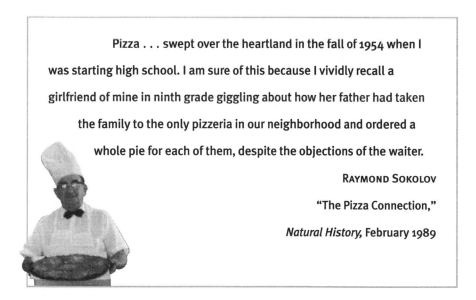

Pizza . . . swept over the heartland in the fall of 1954 when I was starting high school. I am sure of this because I vividly recall a girlfriend of mine in ninth grade giggling about how her father had taken the family to the only pizzeria in our neighborhood and ordered a whole pie for each of them, despite the objections of the waiter.

RAYMOND SOKOLOV

"The Pizza Connection,"

Natural History, February 1989

HOTEL SANTA LUCIA

filled pizzas

One of the best things about writing this book was rediscovering some of the traditional filled pizzas our families made years ago that we had all but forgotten. For Charles it was New Year's Eve Pasta Fritta (page 134), little pan-fried cakes of pizza dough stuffed with anchovies and cheese, which his aunts used to make. For Michele it was Grandma's Baccalà Pizza (page 106), which she could not abide as a child but finds irresistible today. It was one of the many dishes her aunt and mother prepared for their Christmas Eve seafood supper.

This chapter contains a variety of these mouthwatering filled pies. Most are made using a standard pizza dough crust enriched with olive oil, while others are made with cornmeal, semolina, or potato crusts. All of these filled pizzas, sometimes called *pizze rustiche,* or rustic pies, are traditional in southern Italy, though they are little known here. Since they are often associated with holidays or feast days, we suspect that they evolved as a way to make everyday fare like vegetables and bread seem more festive.

The dough for these pizzas is rolled out with a rolling pin so that they will have a better shape. Filled pizzas are great for parties and picnics. You can even freeze slices of filled pizza, well wrapped in plastic and aluminum foil. They reheat well in the oven at a low temperature.

double-crust pizza dough

makes enough for one 12-inch double-crust pizza

1 envelope active dry yeast (2$^1/_2$ teaspoons)
1$^1/_3$ cups warm water (105° to 115°F)
3$^1/_2$ to 4 cups unbleached all-purpose flour
1 teaspoon salt
2 tablespoons olive oil

1. Sprinkle the yeast over the water. Let stand 1 minute, or until the yeast is creamy. Stir until the yeast dissolves.

2. In a large bowl, combine the 3$^1/_2$ cups flour and the salt. Add the yeast mixture and the oil and stir until a soft dough forms. Turn the dough out onto a lightly floured surface and knead, adding more flour if necessary, until smooth and elastic, about 10 minutes.

3. Lightly coat a large bowl with oil. Place the dough in the bowl, turning it to oil the top. Cover with plastic wrap. Place in a warm, draft-free place and let rise until doubled in bulk, about 1$^1/_2$ hours.

4. Flatten the dough with your fist. Cut the dough into 2 pieces and shape the pieces into balls. Dust the tops with flour.

5. Place the balls on a floured surface and cover each with plastic wrap, allowing room for the dough to expand. Let rise 1 hour, or until doubled.

double-crust semolina dough

makes enough for one 12-inch double-crust pizza

1 envelope active dry yeast ($2^{1}/_{2}$ teaspoons)

$1^{1}/_{3}$ cups warm water (105° to 115°F)

2 cups fine semolina flour

$1^{1}/_{2}$ to 2 cups unbleached all-purpose flour

1 teaspoon salt

2 tablespoons olive oil

1. Sprinkle the yeast over the water. Let stand $1^{1}/_{2}$ minute, or until the yeast is creamy. Stir until the yeast is dissolved.

2. In a large bowl, blend the semolina flour with $1^{1}/_{2}$ cups of the all-purpose flour and the salt. Add the yeast mixture and the oil and stir until a soft dough forms. Turn the dough out onto a lightly floured surface and knead until smooth, adding the remaining all-purpose flour as necessary.

3. Oil a large bowl and add the dough, turning it once or twice to oil the top. Cover with plastic wrap and leave in a warm, draft-free place to rise until doubled in bulk, 60 to 90 minutes.

4. Flatten the dough with your fist. Cut the dough into 2 pieces and shape the pieces into balls. Dust the tops with flour.

5. Place the balls on a floured surface and cover each with plastic wrap, allowing room for the dough to expand. Let rise 1 hour, or until doubled.

christmas eve pizza

PIZZA DI SCAROLA / *serves 8*

*M*ichele's mother used to make *pizza di scarola* every year for Christmas Eve. Instead of using a yeast dough, she made it with a lard pie crust, or *pasta frolla*, generously seasoned with black pepper. She fried the pie in a big, heavy, cast-iron skillet. Flipping the pie over was difficult, but she always managed to do it perfectly.

Pizza di scarola is still very popular in Naples today, not just for Christmas but all year round. This version, which we tasted in Italy, is different from Michele's mom's, since it is made with raisins and pine nuts in the filling and baked in a double-crust pizza dough.

> **2 pounds escarole**
> **Salt**
> **¼ cup olive oil**
> **3 large garlic cloves, finely chopped**
> **Pinch of crushed red pepper**
> **1 can (2 ounces) anchovy fillets, drained**
> **3 tablespoons chopped capers**
> **½ cup dark raisins**
> **½ cup pine nuts**
> **1 recipe Double-Crust Pizza Dough (page 100)**

1. Trim the escarole, removing any bruised or brown leaves and cutting off the stem ends. Separate the bunches into leaves. Wash the leaves in several changes of cool water, paying special attention to the white rib in the center where soil collects. In a large pot combine the escarole with 1 cup water and 1 teaspoon salt. Cover and cook over medium heat until tender, about 15 minutes. Drain well and let cool. Remove the excess water from the escarole by wrapping it in a dish towel and squeezing it firmly. Coarsely chop the escarole.

2. In a large skillet, heat the oil over medium heat. Stir in the garlic, red pepper, anchovies, and capers, mashing the anchovies with the back of a spoon. Add the escarole and stir well. Reduce the heat to low and cook, stirring occasionally, about 10 minutes. Add the raisins, pine nuts, and salt to taste. Let cool.

3. Preheat the oven to 425°F. Oil a large baking sheet or a 12-inch pizza pan.

4. With a rolling pin, roll out 1 piece of dough to a 12-inch circle on a lightly floured surface. Transfer the dough to the prepared pan. Spread the filling evenly in the center of the dough, leaving a ½-inch border all around. Roll out the remaining dough to a 12-inch circle. Place the circle over the filling, stretching it gently to meet the edge of the bottom circle. Press the edges of the dough together firmly to seal. With a small, sharp knife, cut several slits in the top of the dough.

5. Bake 35 to 40 minutes, or until browned and crisp. To serve hot, transfer the pizza to a cutting board and cut into wedges. To serve at room temperature, slide the pizza onto a rack to cool.

san vitú's pizza

*t*he nuns of the convent of Saint Vito in Palermo, Sicily, were known for their delicious *sfinciune,* a double-crust pizza. The sisters made several different types of stuffings, but this filling of ground beef, onion, and peas seems most typical. A sprinkling of bread crumbs on top gives the finished pie a nice toasty crunch.

1 large onion, chopped

1 teaspoon fennel seeds

2 tablespoons olive oil

8 ounces ground beef

1 cup chopped tomatoes

2 tablespoons chopped fresh parsley

Salt and freshly ground black pepper

1 cup frozen peas

8 ounces chopped caciocavallo or mozzarella, plus 2 tablespoons grated pecorino Romano

1 recipe Double-Crust Pizza Dough (page 100)

1 egg yolk, blended with 1 tablespoon water

¼ cup plain bread crumbs

1. In a large skillet, cook the onion and fennel seeds in the oil 5 minutes, or until the onion is tender. Add the meat and cook, stirring frequently, until browned, about 10 minutes. Stir in the tomatoes, parsley, and salt and pepper to taste. Cook until thickened, about 5 minutes. Stir in the peas and cook 5 minutes more. Remove from the heat and let cool. Stir in the cheeses.

2. Preheat the oven to 425°F. Oil a 12-inch pizza pan or a large baking sheet.

3. With a rolling pin, roll out 1 piece of dough to a 12-inch circle on a lightly floured surface. Transfer the dough to the prepared pan. Spread the filling evenly in the center of the dough, leaving a ¹/₂-inch border all around. Roll out the remaining dough to a 12-inch circle. Place the circle over the filling, stretching it gently to meet the edge of the bottom circle. Crimp the edges with your fingers, lifting the bottom edge over the top. Press the edges of the dough together firmly to seal.

4. Brush the top with the egg wash. Sprinkle with bread crumbs. With a small, sharp knife, cut several slits in the top of the dough.

5. Bake 35 to 40 minutes, or until browned and crisp. To serve hot, transfer the pizza to a cutting board and cut into wedges. To serve at room temperature, slide the pizza onto a rack to cool.

If the dough for filled pizzas or calzoni gets too dry to stick together or is slicked with oil, brush the border very lightly with water before sealing. Do not use too much water or the crust will be damp and doughy. Press the edges together firmly and let the pizza or calzoni stand 3 to 5 minutes before baking.

When making filled pizzas and calzoni, avoid getting oil on the border of the dough. The oil may prevent the dough from sealing properly and the filling will leak out as it bakes.

grandma's baccalà pizza

PIZZA DI BACCALÀ DELLA NONNA / *serves 8*

*b*efore canning and refrigeration were invented, it was impossible to keep fish fresh. Since Catholics were not permitted to eat meat on Fridays and holy days, dried salted stockfish, called *stoccofisso* or *pesce stocco,* and salt cod *(baccalà)* became popular meat alternatives in Italy.

Stockfish is cod or a similar dried fish. It originated in Scandinavia, where the cold winter winds were perfect for drying and preserving the freshly caught fish. Baccalà is also made from cod, though instead of, or sometimes in addition to being dried, the fish are filleted and salted. Because the fish are cooked in similar ways, the names pesce stocco and baccalà are sometimes used interchangeably in Italy. However, baccalà is much easier to work with and much more likeable. Pesce stocco has a stronger flavor. This pizza can also be made with fresh fish fillets, although it will not be quite as interesting.

Michele's aunt, Millie Castagliola, reminded her that she used to prepare this recipe every Christmas Eve. Aunt Millie learned to make it from her mother, a native of Sicily, who brought the recipe with her when she came to this country. Michele, her sister Annette, and cousins Rosie and Mike hated the pie because of the smell of the stockfish, which can be pretty overwhelming. Funny how tastes change—now we love it!

Stockfish can be found in many Italian, Hispanic, West Indian, and Scandinavian markets. In its dried form, it is so hard and stiff that it looks like a wooden plank and it keeps practically forever. If you do use it, look for large, creamy yellow pieces. Flex the pieces when you change the soaking water to help them soften. Stockfish is pretty smelly even as it soaks, so if you can keep it covered, do so, or better yet, isolate it.

Baccalà seems to be more widely available, or your fishmonger can probably order it for you. Since it is salted but not completely dried, it is perishable and needs to be refrigerated. The soaking treatment is the same, although it does not need more than a day or two to eliminate the salt. To make sure that the baccalà is sufficiently desalted, taste the soaking water before cooking the fish.

> **1 pound stockfish or baccalà, or fresh cod fillets**
> **Salt**
> **3 medium onions, thinly sliced (about 3 cups)**
> **3 celery ribs, thinly sliced (about 2 cups)**
> **¹/₄ cup olive oil**
> **2 garlic cloves, finely chopped**
> **2 cups canned tomatoes with their juice**
> **Pinch of crushed red pepper**
> **¹/₂ cup sliced green olives**
> **2 tablespoons drained capers**
> **1 recipe Double-Crust Pizza Dough (page 100)**

1. If you are using fresh fish, skip to step 4. If using stockfish, begin a week before serving. Place the fish in a pan of cold water in the refrigerator, turning it and changing the water at least twice a day. The aroma will be very strong, so keep the pan covered. As it begins to soften, flex or bend the fish with your hands to help it along. When it is completely puffy, light colored, and softened, it is ready to be cooked. For salt cod or baccalà, place the pieces in a large bowl of cold water. Change the water at least twice a day, for 1 to 3 days, or until the water no longer tastes salty.

2. Bring 4 quarts of water to boiling. Add the fish and salt to taste. Reduce the heat to low. Simmer the stockfish or baccalà until very tender. Drain the fish and cool it slightly. With your fingers, remove the skin and bones. Cut or break the fish into bite-size pieces.

3. In a large saucepan, cook the onions and celery in the oil over medium heat until the onions are tender and golden, about 10 minutes. Stir in the garlic and cook 1 minute more. Add the tomatoes and red pepper and cook until the sauce is thick, 20 to 30 minutes. Add the olives and capers and cook 5 minutes.

4. Add the fish to the sauce and simmer 10 minutes. Taste for salt. Let cool.

5. Preheat the oven to 425°F. Oil a 12-inch pizza pan or a large baking sheet.

6. On a lightly floured surface, roll out half the dough to a 12-inch circle. Drape the dough loosely over the rolling pin and center the dough in the prepared pan. Spread with the filling, leaving a ½-inch border all around. Roll out the remaining dough to a 12-inch circle. Place it over the filling. Press the edges together firmly to seal, lifting the bottom layer over the top at 1-inch intervals to form a braided edge. With a small knife or sharp scissors, make 6 to 8 slits in the top of the dough to allow the steam to escape.

7. Bake the pizza 35 to 40 minutes, or until browned and crisp. Slide the pizza onto a rack to cool. Serve warm or at room temperature.

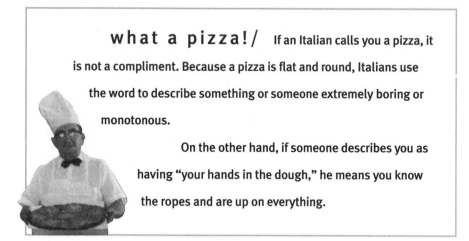

what a pizza!/ If an Italian calls you a pizza, it is not a compliment. Because a pizza is flat and round, Italians use the word to describe something or someone extremely boring or monotonous.

On the other hand, if someone describes you as having "your hands in the dough," he means you know the ropes and are up on everything.

leek and cheese pizza

PIZZA DI PORRI / *serves 8*

*W*e sampled several variations of this pizza in Apulia, the heel of the Italian boot. Some contained fish, and some had olives, but tender leeks were the primary ingredient. Make sure to use a sharp provolone for the best flavor.

> **2 bunches leeks (about 2 pounds)**
> **3 tablespoons olive oil**
> **1 recipe Double-Crust Pizza Dough (page 100)**
> **8 ounces sharp provolone, thinly sliced**

1. Trim the leeks, removing the root end and any bruised outer leaves. Trim off all but 1 inch of the green tops. Cut the leeks in half lengthwise, and rinse them well under cold water, getting in between the leaves. Slice the leeks crosswise into $1/2$-inch pieces. You should have about 3 cups.

2. In a large skillet, heat the oil over medium-low heat. Add the leeks and cover the pan. Cook, stirring occasionally, until the leeks are tender but not browned, about 5 minutes. Remove from the heat and let cool.

3. Preheat the oven to 450°F. Oil a large baking sheet or a 12-inch pizza pan.

4. On a lightly floured surface, roll out 1 piece of dough to a 12-inch circle. Drape the dough over the rolling pin and transfer it to the prepared pan.

5. Spread the filling evenly over the dough, leaving a $1/2$-inch border. Arrange the cheese over the leeks.

6. Roll out the remaining dough to a 12-inch circle. Place the circle over the filling, stretching it gently to meet the bottom edge. Press the edges together to seal. Turn the bottom edge over the top and pinch firmly. With a small, sharp knife, cut several slits in the top of the dough.

7. Bake 35 to 40 minutes, or until browned and crisp. Transfer to a wire rack to cool at least 10 minutes before cutting. Serve warm or at room temperature.

mushroom filled pizza

PIZZA RIPIENA CON I FUNGHI / *serves 8*

*t*he combination of ingredients in the filling for this pizza intrigued us when we read about it in *Il libro d'oro della cucina e dei vini di Calabria e Basilicata (The Golden Book of Food and Wine of Calabria and Basilicata)* by Ottavio Cavalcanti. Hard-cooked eggs are used in many unexpected ways in southern Italy, such as in pasta dishes or as a stuffing for meat loaf or *braciole*. They add creaminess to this pizza filling and bring together the intense flavors of the other ingredients.

Soppressata is a short, wide salami made with ground pork, garlic, cracked black pepper, and other spices. If you can't find it, substitute another firm salami with similar seasonings.

> **1 package (10 to 12 ounces) white mushrooms**
> **2 tablespoons olive oil**
> **2 garlic cloves, finely chopped**
> **1 tablespoon chopped fresh parsley**
> **Salt**
> **1 recipe Double-Crust Pizza Dough (page 100)**
> **2 hard-cooked eggs, peeled and sliced**
> **4 ounces soppressata or similar salami, thinly sliced and**
>   **cut into strips**
> **4 ounces fresh mozzarella, thinly sliced**

1. Wipe the mushrooms with a damp cloth or wash them quickly under cold running water. Trim a thin slice off the base. Halve or quarter the mushrooms if large.

2. In a medium saucepan, heat the oil over medium heat. Add the mushrooms and cook, stirring frequently, 10 minutes, or until the mushroom liquid has evaporated. Stir in the garlic, parsley, and salt to taste. Cook until the mushrooms are lightly browned. Remove the mushrooms from the heat and let cool slightly.

3. Oil a 12-inch pizza pan. Preheat the oven to 425°F.

4. On a lightly floured surface, roll out 1 piece of the dough to a 12-inch circle. Drape the dough over the rolling pin and center it in the pan. Spread the mushrooms in the pan, leaving a ½-inch border all around. Place the eggs, salami, and cheese on top.

5. Roll out the remaining piece of dough to a 12-inch circle. Drape it over the pin and center it on top of the filling. Press the edges of the dough together firmly to seal, folding the bottom layer over the top at 1-inch intervals to form a braided edge. Cut several small slits in the surface of the dough to allow steam to escape.

6. Bake the pie 35 to 40 minutes, or until the crust is golden brown and crisp. Remove from the oven and cool 10 minutes. Slide the pie onto a cutting board if serving hot, or onto a rack to cool completely. Serve hot or at room temperature.

spicy calabrese pizza

PIZZA CALABRESE / *serves 8*

*C*alabria, in the South of Italy, is one of the few regions where people like their food spicy hot. At La Locanda di Alia, a lovely inn and restaurant in Castrovillari, near Cosenza, we tasted some typical dishes. When our host inquired how we liked the food, Michele told him that the combined flavors of the fresh chiles, vegetables, and cheese reminded her of Mexican cooking. He was a little taken aback at first, then sagely replied, "Of course, poor people everywhere learn how to make good-tasting food with just a few simple ingredients."

Calabria historically has been one of the poorest regions of Italy, though it is much more prosperous now than it once was. Fresh and dried chiles are used to add flavor to many foods. We ate cheese and salami spiced with dried chiles, pickled vegetables marinated with chiles, and even potatoes sautéed with chiles (the recipe is in Michele's book *A Fresh Taste of Italy*).

There is not a lot of filling in this pizza, but what there is is so flavorful you do not need more. If you prefer a less spicy filling, you can substitute bell peppers for all or part of the chiles. When handling chiles, remember to protect your hands by wearing latex gloves, or just slip your hands into disposable plastic sandwich bags.

> **4 ounces mild or hot chiles**
> **1 large fresh tomato, or 1 cup drained, canned tomatoes**
> **3 tablespoons olive oil**
> **8 anchovies, drained and chopped**
> **Pinch of salt**
> **1 recipe Double-Crust Pizza Dough (page 100)**

1. Remove the stems and seeds from the chiles. Cut the chiles into thin strips. Cut the tomato in half through the stem. Remove the stem end and squeeze the tomato to eliminate the seeds. Chop the tomato coarsely.

2. In a medium skillet, heat the oil over medium heat. Add the chiles and tomato, and cook 15 minutes, or until tender and most of the juices have evaporated. Stir in the anchovies and salt. Remove from the heat and let cool.

3. Oil a 12-inch pizza pan. Preheat the oven to 425°F.

4. On a lightly floured surface, roll out 1 piece of the dough to a 12-inch circle. Drape the dough over the rolling pin and center it in the pan. Spread the filling over the dough, leaving a ¹/₂-inch border all around.

5. Roll out the remaining piece of dough to a 12-inch circle. Drape it over the pin and center it on top of the filling. Press the edges of the dough together firmly to seal, folding the bottom layer over the top at 1-inch intervals to form a braided edge. Cut several small slits in the surface of the dough to allow steam to escape.

6. Bake the pie 40 minutes, or until the crust is golden brown and crisp. Remove from the oven and cool 10 minutes. Slide the pie onto a cutting board if serving hot, or onto a rack to cool completely. Serve hot or at room temperature.

sausage cauliflower pie

PIZZA DI SALSICCIA E CAVOLFIORE / *serves 8*

*C*auliflower is rather bland in color and flavor, but Sicilian cooks know how to turn those drawbacks into assets. Cauliflower's mild taste is the perfect foil for flavorful tomatoes, olives, and garlic. We have eaten Sicilian-style pasta with cauliflower, tomato sauce, anchovies, and bread crumbs; and with cauliflower, saffron, raisins, and pine nuts. Some cooks stew cauliflower with olives and wine, while others fry it in a light batter until crispy and golden. All it takes is a little imagination to turn a ho-hum vegetable into something sensational.

In this Sicilian-style pie the simple flavor of cauliflower is enhanced by fennel-scented pork sausages, tomatoes, garlic, and olives.

1/2 small head cauliflower (about 1 pound), trimmed
and cut into flowers

Salt

2 tablespoons olive oil

8 ounces Italian-style pork sausages with
fennel seeds, skins removed

2 garlic cloves, sliced

1 large tomato, peeled, seeded, and chopped (1 cup)

1 cup imported black olives, pitted and chopped

Freshly ground black pepper

1 recipe Double-Crust Semolina Dough
(page 101)

1 egg yolk, blended with 1 tablespoon water

1. Bring a large saucepan of water to boiling. Add the cauliflower and salt to taste. Cook until the cauliflower is tender when pierced with a fork, about 8 minutes. Drain the cauliflower and chop it into ½-inch pieces.

2. In a large skillet, heat the oil over medium heat. Add the sausages and the garlic and cook, stirring often to break up the lumps, until browned, about 10 minutes. Add the tomato and cook 5 minutes more. Stir in the cauliflower and olives, and remove from the heat. Season to taste with salt and pepper and let cool.

3. Preheat the oven to 425°F. Oil a large baking sheet or a 12-inch round pizza pan.

4. On a lightly floured surface, roll out 1 piece of the dough to a 12-inch circle. Place it on the prepared baking sheet or fit it into the pizza pan. Spoon the cauliflower mixture over the dough, leaving a ½-inch border all around. Roll out the remaining dough. Using the rolling pin to help you lift it, place the dough over the filling. Firmly pinch the edges of the dough together to seal. Brush the surface with the egg wash. With a knife, make several small slits in the top of the dough. Bake 35 to 40 minutes, or until golden brown and crisp.

5. Slide the baked pie onto a cutting board. Let cool 10 minutes before slicing into wedges. Serve warm or at room temperature.

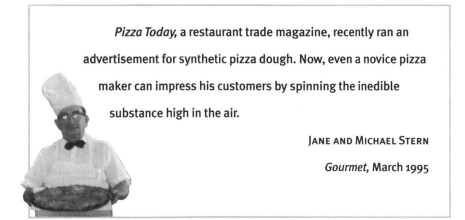

Pizza Today, a restaurant trade magazine, recently ran an advertisement for synthetic pizza dough. Now, even a novice pizza maker can impress his customers by spinning the inedible substance high in the air.

JANE AND MICHAEL STERN

Gourmet, March 1995

cornmeal and broccoli rabe pizza

PIZZA DI POLENTA / *serves 8*

*b*roccoli rabe must be blanched in boiling water to tenderize it and tame the vegetable's bitter edge. If you prefer, substitute other greens for the broccoli rabe, such as spinach, kale, or escarole. Since spinach and escarole have a lot of moisture, make sure to drain them well before filling the pizza or the crust may become soggy. The golden yellow cornmeal crust and deep green vegetable filling makes this pizza from southern Italy as delicious to look at as it is to eat.

DOUGH

1 envelope active dry yeast (2^1/$_2$ teaspoons)

1^1/$_2$ cups warm water (105° to 115°F)

2^1/$_2$ to 3 cups unbleached all-purpose flour

2 cups fine yellow cornmeal

1 teaspoon salt

^{1}/$_4$ cup olive oil

FILLING

1^1/$_2$ pounds broccoli rabe

Salt

3 tablespoons olive oil

3 large garlic cloves, sliced

Pinch of crushed red pepper

4 to 6 anchovy fillets

1. To make the dough, sprinkle the yeast over the water. Let stand 1 minute, or until the yeast is creamy. Stir until the yeast is dissolved.

2. In a large bowl, combine 2^1/$_2$ cups of the flour, the cornmeal, and salt. Add the dissolved yeast and the oil. Stir until a soft dough forms. Turn the dough out onto a lightly floured surface and knead, adding more flour if necessary, until the dough is smooth and elastic, about 10 minutes.

3. Lightly coat a large bowl with oil. Place the dough in the bowl, turning it once to oil the top. Cover with plastic wrap. Put the bowl in a warm, draft-free place until doubled in bulk, about 2 hours.

4. Flatten the dough with your fist. Cut the dough into 2 pieces and shape the pieces into balls. Dust the tops with flour.

5. Place the balls on a floured surface and cover each with plastic wrap, allowing room for the dough to expand. Let rise 1 hour, or until doubled.

6. To make the filling, trim off the base of the broccoli rabe. Discard any tough stems or yellowed leaves. Cut the broccoli rabe into 1-inch lengths.

7. Bring a large pot of water to boiling. Add the broccoli rabe and salt to taste. Cook until tender, about 5 minutes. Drain.

8. In the same pot, heat the oil over medium heat. Add the garlic and red pepper. Cook until the garlic is golden, about 1 minute. Stir in the anchovies. Add the broccoli rabe and stir well. Add salt to taste. Set aside and let cool.

9. Preheat the oven to 450°F. Oil a 12-inch pizza pan.

10. Roll out 1 piece of the dough to make a 12-inch circle. Place the dough in the prepared pan. Spread the filling over the dough, leaving a ½-inch border all around. Roll out the remaining dough to a 12-inch circle and place it over the filling. Pinch the edges firmly to seal the dough. With a small knife, cut several slits in the surface of the dough. Brush the top with oil.

11. Bake 25 to 30 minutes, or until crisp and golden brown. Slide the pizza onto a cutting board and let cool 10 minutes. Cut into wedges to serve.

sausage and greens potato-crust pizza

PIZZA DI SALSICCIA E VERDURA / *serves 8*

*O*ne of our favorite places to buy pork products is Calabria Pork Store on Arthur Avenue in the Bronx, New York. There must be thousands of salamis hanging from the ceiling to dry and age, each row neatly marked with the date they were made. The fresh pork sausages are flavored with pecorino Romano cheese and parsley, chiles, or broccoli rabe. All of their sausages are meaty and full of flavor, and when cooked, burst with delicious juices.

The potato and semolina crust of this double-crust pizza is a delicious match for the tasty filling of sausage, greens, ricotta, and ricotta salata, a pressed and lightly salted version of the fresh cheese.

POTATO-SEMOLINA DOUGH

1 medium potato (6 ounces) or ¾ cup leftover mashed potato

1 package active dry yeast

½ cup warm water (105° to 115°F)

½ cup warm milk

2 cups unbleached all-purpose flour, plus more for rolling out the dough

1 cup fine semolina flour

1½ teaspoons salt

FILLING

1 tablespoon olive oil

8 ounces Italian sausages, skinned

2 cups chopped cooked broccoli or other greens, such as Swiss chard or spinach

1 pound or one 15-ounce container ricotta (2 cups)

½ cup chopped ricotta salata (about 2 ounces)

Olive oil, for brushing the top

1. To make the dough, place the potato in a small pot with cold water to cover. Bring the water to boiling and cook until the potato is tender when pierced with a knife. Drain and cool slightly. Peel the potato and mash it with a fork. You should have about ³/₄ cup.

2. In a bowl, sprinkle the yeast over the water and let stand 1 minute, or until softened. Stir until dissolved. Add the milk. Stir in the mashed potato.

3. In a large bowl, combine the all-purpose flour, the semolina, and the salt.

4. Add the potato mixture to the dry ingredients. Stir until a soft dough forms. Turn the dough out onto a lightly floured surface and knead until smooth and elastic, about 10 minutes, adding more flour as needed. This dough should remain sticky.

5. Oil a large bowl. Add the dough, turning it over to oil the top. Let rise in a warm, draft-free place 1 hour, or until doubled in bulk.

6. Make your hand into a fist and punch the dough down to eliminate air bubbles. Cut it into 2 pieces and shape each piece into a ball. Dust the tops with flour and cover loosely with plastic wrap, allowing enough room for the dough to expand. Let rise 1 hour, or until doubled.

7. To make the filling, in a medium skillet, heat the oil over medium heat. Add the sausage meat, stirring often to break up lumps. Cook until the meat is lightly browned, about 10 minutes. Drain off excess fat. Let cool.

8. In a bowl, combine the sausage, broccoli, ricotta, and ricotta salata.

9. Preheat the oven to 425°F. Oil a 12-inch pizza pan or a large baking sheet.

10. On a lightly floured surface, roll out 1 piece of the dough to a 12-inch circle. Drape the dough loosely over the rolling pin and center it in the prepared pan. Spread with the filling, leaving a ¹/₂-inch border all around. Roll out the remaining dough to a 12-inch circle. Place it over the filling. Press the edges together firmly to seal, folding the bottom layer over the top to form a braided edge. With a small knife or sharp scissors, make 6 to 8 slits in the top of the dough to allow the steam to escape.

11. Brush the top of the pizza with oil. Bake 40 minutes, or until browned and crisp. Remove from the oven and cool 10 minutes. Serve hot or at room temperature.

cauliflower and broccoli pizza

PIZZA RUSTICA DI CAVOLFIORE E BROCCOLI / *serves 8*

*p*izza rustica, rustic pie, is a name given by Neapolitans to many types of stuffed savory pizzas. The inspiration for this particular filling came about when Michele was working on an article on pizza for *Eating Well* magazine. The editors did not feel that cauliflower was interesting enough in itself, so Michele suggested combining it with broccoli, a vegetable with more color and flavor. We bake this pizza in a 10-inch springform pan for added depth, but it can also be baked in a 12-inch pizza pan.

**1 recipe Double-Crust Pizza Dough (page 100), prepared
    through step 3**
4 cups broccoli florets
4 cups cauliflower florets
Salt
6 large garlic cloves, sliced
Pinch of crushed red pepper
¹/₄ cup olive oil
1 can (2 ounces) anchovy fillets, drained
¹/₂ cup imported black olives, such as Gaeta

1. Cut the dough into 2 pieces, one slightly larger than the other. Press the dough down to squeeze out the air bubbles. Shape each piece into a ball. Place the balls several inches apart on a lightly floured surface, such as a cutting board. Cover with plastic wrap and let rise until doubled, about 1 hour.

2. Bring a large pot of water to boiling. Add the broccoli, cauliflower, and salt to taste. Cook the vegetables until crisp tender, about 5 minutes. Drain. Chop coarsely.

3. In a large skillet, cook the garlic and red pepper in the oil over low heat until golden. Add the anchovies and stir until dissolved.

4. Stir in the broccoli, cauliflower, and olives. Add salt to taste. Set aside and let cool.

5. Preheat the oven to 425°F. Oil a 10 × 2-inch springform pan.

6. With a rolling pin, roll out the larger piece of dough on a lightly floured surface to make a 14-inch circle. Arrange the dough in the prepared pan, patting it up the sides. Spread the filling in the pan, pressing it down with the back of a spoon.

7. Roll out the remaining dough to a 10-inch circle and place it over the filling. Pinch the edges firmly to seal the dough. With scissors or a small knife, cut several slits in the surface of the dough.

8. Bake 35 to 40 minutes, or until crisp and golden brown. Remove the pizza from the pan and let cool 10 minutes. Cut into wedges and serve warm.

pizza spinning / Old-time variety shows often featured an agile acrobat twirling plates with his nose while juggling glassware and riding a unicycle. It is amazing and fun to watch, but spinning plates is no more essential to setting the table than spinning pizza dough is to making a good pizza. Pizza spinning is more about showmanship than making good pizza. The custom probably began when a bored pizzaiolo with a flair for the dramatic tossed his dough in the air as a novel means of stretching it. If done properly, spinning will stretch the dough somewhat, but it is terribly messy if done incorrectly and not at all necessary to getting an evenly shaped pie. Try it if you like, but have an extra batch of dough on hand in case the spun dough does not land where it should.

eggplant and provolone filled pizza

PIZZA RIPIENA DI MELANZANE / *serves 8*

*W*e consider ourselves fortunate to have several old-fashioned Italian-style *latticini* near where we live in Brooklyn. A latticino is a store that specializes in cheeses, though usually other foods like pasta, cured meats, and olives are sold as well. The air is filled with mouthwatering aromas from the herbs and garlic, and from the salamis hanging to dry, plus the woodsy aroma of freshly smoked mozzarella and the sharp, tangy smell of provolone. When we were kids, we were fascinated by the golden balls of provolone cheeses that were suspended with twine from the rafters just out of our reach, looking like so many little basketballs. A favorite lunch then—and now—is a wedge of provolone, roasted peppers dressed with garlic and good olive oil, and some crisp Italian bread.

Provolone is made in a similar manner to mozzarella, except provolone is aged. Naturally, the older the provolone, the sharper the flavor, but for this recipe, you can use whatever kind, mild or sharp, that suits your taste.

2 medium eggplants (about 2 pounds)

Salt

Olive oil

**1 pound ripe tomatoes, peeled, seeded, and chopped,
   or 1 cup canned tomatoes, drained and chopped**

6 ounces provolone, chopped or coarsely grated

¼ cup chopped fresh basil

Freshly ground black pepper

1 recipe Double-Crust Semolina Dough (page 101)

1. Cut the eggplant into 1-inch cubes. Layer the pieces in a large colander, sprinkling each layer with salt. Place the colander over a plate. Let the eggplant stand 1 hour to drain off the liquid. Rinse the eggplant well under cool running water to eliminate the salt. Squeeze the eggplant in a towel until dry.

2. In a deep saucepan, heat about 2 inches of oil. Fry the eggplant in small batches until browned on all sides. Drain on paper towels.

3. In a bowl, mix together the eggplant, tomatoes, cheese, and basil. Season to taste with salt and pepper.

4. Oil a 12-inch pizza pan. Preheat the oven to 425°F.

5. On a lightly floured surface, roll out 1 piece of dough with a rolling pin to a 12-inch circle.

6. Arrange the dough in the prepared pan. Spread the filling over the dough, leaving a 1/2-inch border all around. Roll out the remaining dough to a 12-inch circle and center it over the filling. Pinch the edges together to seal. With a small knife, make several slits in the top layer of dough to allow steam to escape.

7. Bake 35 to 40 minutes, or until crisp and golden brown. Slide the pizza onto a cutting board and let cool 10 minutes. Serve hot or at room temperature. Cut into wedges.

HOTEL SANTA LUCIA
NAPOLI

calzoni and other savory turnovers

a calzone is nothing more than a flat pizza that has been folded in half so that the topping is sealed inside the dough instead of on top, something like a savory turnover. Because of their shape, these turnovers are called calzoni, meaning trouser legs.

Calzoni keep well and are perfectly portable. Mini calzoni are great for parties. You can make both large and small calzoni in advance, and keep them warm in a 250°F oven for up to an hour. Or cool them completely on racks, and wrap and refrigerate them until needed. Reheat the calzoni on a baking sheet in a 350°F oven for 10 to 15 minutes. In Naples calzoni are often fried, though in this country, they are usually baked. If you like, serve calzoni with a spoonful of tomato sauce on top.

The fillings included here are just suggestions. Use whatever cheeses, meats, and vegetables are available. Don't overstuff the calzoni, though, or they are likely to leak.

Dora's Panzerotti (page 132) and New Year's Eve Pasta Fritta (page 134) are turnovers similar to little calzoni.

calzoni

makes 4

*Y*ou can use the same dough for both filled pizzas and calzoni. Because it contains a little olive oil, this dough stays a bit moister during the long baking time. For fried calzoni, which cook much quicker, use either this dough or the basic pizza dough without oil.

1 recipe Double-Crust Pizza Dough (page 100),
prepared through step 3

1. With your fist, punch the dough down. Divide the dough into 4 pieces. Shape each piece into a ball. Place the balls several inches apart on a lightly floured surface, such as a cutting board. Cover loosely with plastic wrap and let rise until doubled in bulk, about 1 hour.

2. Preheat the oven to 425°F. Oil 2 large baking sheets.

3. On a lightly floured surface, roll out the dough with a rolling pin into four 9-inch circles. Drape the circles over the rolling pin and transfer them to the baking sheets, reshaping them as needed.

4. Spoon an equal portion of one of the fillings that follow on half of each circle, leaving a ½-inch border for sealing. Fold over the unfilled half and press firmly to seal. Then fold the border over and seal again at 1-inch intervals to make a braided edge.

5. Cut a ½-inch slit in the top of each calzone to allow the steam to escape.

6. Bake 35 to 40 minutes, or until crisp and browned. Slide onto a rack to cool 5 minutes before slicing.

mini calzoni (makes 16) In step 1 cut each ball of dough into 4 pieces. Roll each piece out into a 4- to 5-inch circle. Place the filling on half of each circle. Seal, slit, and bake as directed.

potato, fennel, and onion calzoni filling

CALZONI DI PATATE E CIPOLLE / *makes enough filling for four 9-inch calzoni*

*g*rowing up in Brooklyn, we enjoyed eating all kinds of ethnic foods. One of our favorite places for lunch was the local Jewish deli, where we feasted on pastrami or brisket sandwiches and crisp, garlicky pickles. For eating on the go, however, there was nothing better than a knish, a hot, doughy pouch packed with onion and black pepper–seasoned mashed potatoes. Just one hot, hearty knish could fill you up for the whole day.

These calzoni remind us of those deli knishes, but with an Italian accent, thanks to the flavor of the fennel seeds. Be sure to slice the potatoes thinly so that they are cooked through.

3 small boiling potatoes, peeled and very thinly sliced (about 1 pound)

2 medium onions, halved and very thinly sliced (about 8 ounces)

2 tablespoons olive oil

1 teaspoon fennel seeds

1 teaspoon coarse salt

1/4 teaspoon freshly ground black pepper

1. In a bowl, toss the vegetables with the oil, fennel seeds, salt, and pepper.

2. Shape, fill, and bake the calzoni as described on page 126.

classic calzoni filling

CALZONI CLASSICI / *makes enough filling for four 9-inch calzoni*

*W*hen Charles was a little boy, he liked nothing better than to be taken to Scarola's, a local Italian restaurant known for its calzoni. He loved to watch the pizzaiolo, who worked behind a glass window, deftly shaping the half-moon–shaped pies filled with cheese and meats. His mother and father ordered both pizza and calzoni, then ate the pizza first so as to give the calzoni, oozing molten cheese like a volcano, a chance to cool down.

1 pound ricotta

8 ounces diced fresh mozzarella

¹/₂ cup grated Parmigiano-Reggiano

4 ounces diced prosciutto or salami

1 tablespoon chopped fresh parsley

1. Combine the cheeses, prosciutto, and parsley.

2. Shape, fill, and bake the calzoni as described on page 126.

california calzoni

CALZONI DI CALIFORNIA / *makes enough filling for four 9-inch calzoni*

*t*he first freelance food article Michele ever wrote was about calzoni, which was inspired by their popularity at Chez Panisse, Alice Waters's innovative
restaurant in Berkeley, California. In the early '80s, the Chez Panisse calzone was all the
rage, and no wonder, since its goat cheese, garlic, and herb stuffing showed how versatile
calzoni can be. This is our version.

6 ounces fresh goat cheese, without rind

1 cup ricotta

1/4 cup freshly grated Parmigiano-Reggiano

1 large garlic clove, minced

2 tablespoons chopped fresh basil

Freshly ground black pepper

4 thin slices prosciutto

1. Combine the cheeses, garlic, basil, and pepper to taste.

2. Shape and fill the calzoni as described on page 126, placing a slice of prosciutto on
top of the cheese mixture.

3. Bake as directed.

sausage and pepper calzoni filling

CALZONI DI SALSICCIA E PEPERONI / *makes enough filling for four*

9-inch calzoni

*C*harles's Uncle Nicky loved sausage and pepper sandwiches. Every Christmas Eve, he would make up a big batch to serve to the family after Midnight Mass. Charles always knew that no matter what time he arrived, Uncle Nicky would have one of his special sandwiches waiting for him. This calzoni filling always makes him think of his uncle's hearty sandwiches.

$^3/_4$ **pound Italian sweet or hot sausages**

3 tablespoons olive oil

2 to 3 medium bell peppers (about 1 pound)

3 medium onions, thinly sliced

Salt and freshly ground black pepper

1. Prick the sausages all over with a fork. Place in a medium skillet with $^1/_2$ inch water. Cover and simmer over moderate heat until the water evaporates, about 20 minutes. Uncover and cook, turning occasionally, until the sausages are browned. Let cool, then cut into $^1/_4$-inch slices.

2. In a large skillet, combine the oil and the peppers. Cook over medium heat 5 minutes. Add the onions and salt and pepper to taste. Cook until the peppers are soft and the onions are lightly browned, 15 to 20 minutes. Remove from the heat and let cool before assembling the calzoni.

3. To fill the calzoni, arrange sausage slices over half of each circle of the dough. Top with the peppers and onions. Bake as directed.

fried calzoni

makes 4 large or 16 mini calzoni

      *S*trolling through the Forcella market in Naples one day, on our way to Pizzeria Da Michele, we came upon two men on a street corner frying calzoni in a makeshift, open-air kitchen. Customers stepped up to their oilcloth-covered table and placed their order. The calzoni maker filled the soft rounds of dough with cheeses, bits of sausage or other meats, and sometimes vegetables, folded and quickly sealed them, then dropped them into a cauldron of boiling oil. His partner cooked the calzoni, turning them once or twice to make sure they were evenly brown, then lifting them out with a large strainer and wrapping them in paper before handing them to the hungry customer. Some requested a dollop of tomato sauce on top. We bought one to share as a snack for about a dollar.

      When making fried calzoni, make sure to use a filling that just needs to be heated, not actually cooked. Fried calzoni are done in only 5 or 6 minutes.

> **Vegetable oil for frying**
> **1 recipe Double-Crust Pizza Dough (page 100) with**
>   **Classic Calzoni Filling (page 128) or goat cheese filling**
>   **(see page 129)**

1. Pour the oil into a 3- to 4-inch deep skillet or a wide saucepan to a depth of about 1 inch. Heat over medium heat until the temperature of the oil reaches 370°F on a frying thermometer, or until a small cube of bread dropped into the oil browns evenly in 1 minute. Using tongs or a metal spatula, carefully slip a calzone into the hot oil. If the pan is wide enough, add a second calzone, but make sure that there is sufficient space for the oil to bubble up without boiling over.

2. Fry the calzoni 2 minutes, or until golden brown on one side. With long metal or wooden tongs, turn the calzoni over and fry the other side, about 2 minutes more. Transfer the calzoni to a baking sheet lined with paper towels to drain. Repeat with the remaining calzoni. Let cool 5 minutes before slicing. Fried calzoni can be eaten immediately or they can be kept warm in a 250°F oven up to 1 hour.

dora's panzerotti

makes 16

*i*n Italy panzerotti can refer either to potato croquettes, to stuffed pizza like calzoni, or to these little fried turnovers from Apulia. This version of panzerotti comes from Dora Marzovilla, whose son Nicola is the owner of i Trulli restaurant in New York, where Charles works as the wine director. In addition to making all of the restaurant's fresh pasta and focaccia, Dora makes batches of these turnovers daily to be served in the restaurant's *enoteca* (wine bar). Golden brown and crisp, they make great snacks or appetizers with a glass of wine.

After making up the panzerotti, let them stand a few minutes before frying them. This helps them to seal better, so that they won't open when placed in the hot oil.

> 3 plum tomatoes (8 ounces) or 1 large tomato
> Salt
> 1 recipe Basic Dough (page 64) or Neapolitan-Style Pizza
>   Dough (page 36)
> 4 ounces fresh mozzarella, cut into sixteen ½-inch sticks
> 1 can (2 ounces) flat anchovy fillets, drained and chopped
> Vegetable oil for deep frying

1. Coarsely chop the tomatoes. Place them in a colander set over a plate and sprinkle with salt. Let drain for 30 minutes.

2. Cut the dough in quarters. Cut each quarter into 4 pieces. Cover the dough with an overturned bowl. On a lightly floured surface, roll out 1 piece of dough to a 4-inch circle. Place 1 teaspoon tomatoes, and a piece each of mozzarella and anchovy to one side of the circle. Fold the other half of the dough over the filling. Press out the air and pinch the edges firmly together to seal. Use a fork to seal them tight.

3. In a deep, heavy saucepan or a deep fryer, heat at least 1 inch of oil to a temperature of 370°F on an frying thermometer, or until a 1-inch piece of bread browns in 1 minute. Carefully slip the panzerotti, a few at a time, into the hot oil. Leave enough room between them so that they do not touch. Turn the panzerotti once or twice and cook until golden brown, about 3 minutes. If necessary, hold the panzerotti under the oil with a metal spoon.

4. Remove the panzerotti with tongs or a slotted spoon. Place them on paper towels to drain. Serve hot. Be careful when you bite into them, as the juices can be very hot.

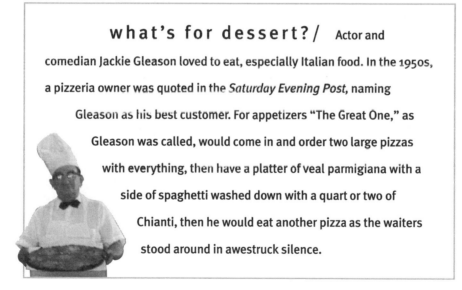

what's for dessert? / Actor and comedian Jackie Gleason loved to eat, especially Italian food. In the 1950s, a pizzeria owner was quoted in the *Saturday Evening Post*, naming Gleason as his best customer. For appetizers "The Great One," as Gleason was called, would come in and order two large pizzas with everything, then have a platter of veal parmigiana with a side of spaghetti washed down with a quart or two of Chianti, then he would eat another pizza as the waiters stood around in awestruck silence.

new year's eve pasta fritta

makes 12

$\mathcal{W}$hen Charles was very young, he lived with his mother and six aunts in his grandmother's house. His father and the other men in the family were away in World War II, so the women doted on the little boy, the first grandchild and nephew, and would make him whatever he wanted to eat, which probably explains why Charles never learned to cook anything.

His favorite treats were these little pan-fried rolls, which his aunt Frieda made for him to celebrate New Year's Eve. He called them *pasta Frieda* instead of *pasta fritta,* meaning fried dough, because he thought they were named for his aunt. These rolls are similar to panzerotti (see page 132), but since they are pan-fried instead of deep-fried, the result is quite different.

> **1 recipe Basic Dough (page 64) or Neapolitan-Style**
> **Pizza Dough (page 36)**
> **1 can (2 ounces) flat anchovy fillets, drained and**
> **cut into pieces**
> **About 4 ounces mozzarella, cut into twelve ½-inch**
> **sticks**
> **Vegetable oil for frying**

1. Divide the dough in half. Cut each half into 6 pieces. Place 1 piece on a lightly floured surface. Cover the remaining pieces with an overturned bowl.

2. Roll out the dough to a circle about 5 inches in diameter. Place a piece of anchovy and a piece of mozzarella in the center of the circle. Lift the edges of the dough together, pressing out the air. Pinch the edges firmly to seal, then flatten the seam. Place the finished cake on a baking sheet sprinkled with flour. Repeat with the remaining ingredients.

3. Pour the oil into a large skillet. It should coat the bottom generously. Heat the oil over medium heat until quite hot. Add the dough pieces, seam side down, a few at a time. Fry the cakes, flattening them with the back of a spatula, until browned, about 2 minutes per side. Drain on paper towels.

4. Fry the remaining dough in the same way. Let the pasta fritta cool slightly before eating. Be careful when you bite into them, since the inside remains very hot while the outside cools.

Pomodoro, Mozzarella, Formaggio e Basilico

MARGHERITA con funghi
Pomodoro, Mozzarella, Formaggio e Basilico

MARGHERITA alla romana
Mozzarella, Acciughe, Pomodoro e Basilico

MARGHERITA con prosciutto e funghi
Pomodoro, Mozzarella, Formaggio e Basilico

MARGHERITA con panna
Pomodoro, Mozzarella, Formaggio, Basilico e Panna

MARGHERITA con filetto pomodorini
Filetto di pomodoro, Fior di latte, Formaggio e Basilico

PIZZA al prosciutto crudo
Pomodoro, Mozzarella, Prosciutto crudo,
Formaggio e Basilico

PIZZA CAPRESE
Pomodoro per insalata, Mozzarella, Basilico ed Origano

PIZZA alla campagnola
Olive, Acciughe, Pomodoro, Capperi, Aglio ed Origano

PIZZA sostanziosa
Pomodoro, Mozzarella, Prosciutto, Uova,
Formaggio e Basilico

PIZZA lasagna
Pomodoro, Mozzarella, Ricotta, Prosciutto, Formaggio e Ba

PIZZA forte
Salame piccante, Peperoni sottolio, Pomodoro,
Peperoncino e Basilico

PIZZA alle 4 stagioni
Campagnola, Marinaresca, Margherita con funghi

PIZZA capricciosa
Mozzarella, Prosciutto, Pomodoro, Funghi,
Olive, Capperi, Formaggio e Basilico

PIZZA con salsiccia e friarielli

**HOTEL SANTA LUCIA
NAPOLI**

regional italian pizzas and flatbreads

*p*izza in one form or another has existed for centuries all over Italy. The Neapolitans elevated pizza making to an art form, but cooks in other regions also make a variety of wonderful pizzas. They are another reflection of the regionality of Italian cooking, just as gnocchi, ravioli, and spaghetti are all pastas even though made with different ingredients in completely different ways.

A Sicilian favorite is sfinciuni, of which there are numerous varieties. Some sfinciuni are covered double-crust pies, while others have only a single crust. One thing that all sfinciuni have in common is that the toppings or fillings are substantial, thick, and hearty with meats, cheeses, anchovies, and vegetables. In fact, some food historians believe that it was sfinciuni that inspired Chicago's deep-dish pizza.

Though some might argue that *farinata* and *piadina* are not pizzas, we include them in this section, since they are close relatives. Both savory flatbreads are eaten hot as snacks, appetizers, or light meals.

A piadina is a tender disk of dough leavened only with baking powder. In Romagna (the easterly portion of Emilia-Romagna), piadine are especially popular snacks at beach resorts along the coast.

Farinata is said to have evolved centuries ago when wheat flour was scarce and expensive. It is easily and speedily made with chickpea flour, olive oil, salt, and water. After a rest, the rather liquid batter is poured into a flat baking pan and browned quickly in a hot oven.

Also included in this chapter is a pizza baked in a pan that is typical of southern Italian home cooking. This recipe was given to us by Charles's uncle Joe, who remembers learning it from his Neapolitan grandfather.

piadina

makes 8

*O*ne summer, a few years ago, we visited the coast of Emilia-Romagna in northern Italy. Because of unusual weather conditions, the shoreline was covered with slimy green algae, and vacationers went elsewhere for their holidays, which meant that all of the hotels were empty and the towns were deserted.

We decided to forgo the beach, but stay in Milano Marittima a few days anyway. We drove through the town and found a hotel with a swimming pool and a pretty garden. The hotel proprietors were so happy and surprised to see us, they would have rolled out a red carpet. We could have our choice of any room. We settled on one with a view of the garden and the street beyond, where we could see the local piadina stand just opening for business. As soon as we settled in, we ran down to get some.

A piadina is a flatbread baked on a griddle, then folded in half, and stuffed. The stuffings include various sautéed greens; cold meats, such as sliced prosciutto, salami, or mortadella; a semisoft cheese like Fontina, or a fresh, creamy cheese called *squacarone*. Italian children prefer their piadine with Nutella—a very sweet hazelnut and chocolate spread, the Italian equivalent of peanut butter. Our friend Hadrian Gallo, an American baseball player who lived in the area for a number of years, remembers having piadina with lemon mayonnaise and cold roast pork. Piadine are usually eaten like sandwiches, but we like to cut them into small wedges to serve as appetizers.

3¹/₂ cups unbleached all-purpose flour

1 teaspoon salt

¹/₂ teaspoon baking powder

1 cup warm water (105° to 115°F)

¹/₄ cup olive oil

1. In a food processor or a heavy-duty mixer, combine the flour, salt, and baking powder. Add the water and oil. Process or mix until the dough is smooth and elastic, about 1 minute. Remove from the machine and knead the dough briefly by hand on a lightly floured surface. Shape the dough into a ball. Let rest covered with a bowl for 20 minutes to 1 hour. (Can also be made up to a day ahead of time. Store the dough in a sealed plastic bag in the refrigerator. Let the dough come to room temperature before proceeding.)

2. Cut the dough into 8 pieces. Cover all but 1 piece with an overturned bowl. On a lightly floured surface, shape the piece into a ball. With a rolling pin, roll out the dough to an 8-inch circle. Place a piece of wax paper on a large dinner plate. Place the circle of dough on top. Roll out the remaining dough, stacking the circles on the plate with a piece of wax paper in between them.

3. Heat a well-seasoned pancake griddle or a nonstick skillet over medium-high heat. Test the temperature by flicking some droplets of water onto the surface. If the water sizzles and evaporates quickly, the griddle is ready. Place a circle of dough on the griddle or skillet. Cook 30 seconds, or until the dough begins to stiffen and turns a golden brown. If it browns too rapidly, reduce the heat slightly. Flip the piadina and brown the other side. The piadina can be served immediately or wrapped in a piece of foil and kept warm in a low oven while you cook the remainder in the same way.

4. To serve, fold a piadina in half and fill it with Mixed Greens with Garlic (recipe follows); sliced prosciutto, mortadella, or salami; a semifirm cheese, such as Fontina Valle d'Aosta or soft fresh goat cheese and arugula; or Nutella.

mixed greens with garlic

makes enough filling for 8 piadina

1½ pounds mixed greens, such as escarole, spinach,
   or Swiss chard
Coarse or kosher salt
3 tablespoons olive oil
2 large garlic cloves, thinly sliced
Pinch of crushed red pepper

1. Trim the greens, discarding any bruised or yellowed leaves. Cut the greens into 2-inch lengths.

2. Bring about 2 quarts of water to boiling. Add the greens and salt to taste. Cook 5 minutes, or until tender. Drain well.

3. Dry the pot and add the oil, garlic, and red pepper. Cook over medium-low heat until the garlic turns golden. Add the greens and stir well. Cover and cook 5 minutes more. Taste for salt. Serve hot or at room temperature.

umbrian-style flatbread

CIACCIA AL PANAIO / *makes 8*

*t*his Umbrian flatbread is similar to Piadina (page 138) except it is made with whole wheat flour as well as white flour. Serve it with any of the fillings for Piadina.

> 2¹/₂ cups unbleached all-purpose flour
>
> 1 cup whole wheat flour
>
> 1 teaspoon salt
>
> ¹/₂ teaspoon baking powder
>
> 1 cup warm water (105° to 115°F)
>
> ¹/₄ cup olive oil

Prepare and bake the dough exactly the same way as for Piadina.

> There is always a good reason for eating a pizza; in winter because the weather is cold, and the sight of the fire crackling on the charcoal stove delights and warms you; in summer because most pizzerie set their tables and chairs in the open and you can breathe the cool evening air.
>
> ALEXANDER LENARD
>
> *The Fine Art of Roman Cooking*

four cheese pizza from the marche

CRESCIA / *serves 8*

*f*our kinds of cheese kneaded into the dough make this pizza, which comes from the Marche region of central Italy, heaven for cheese lovers. Some of the cheese is grated, while some is chopped into bits for an interesting texture. The dough is made with a starter for extra flavor. This pizza makes a great appetizer or serve it for lunch or a light supper with a big tossed salad. Search out Rosso Conero, a fine red wine from the Marche, to serve alongside.

STARTER

1 package active dry yeast or 2 teaspoons instant yeast

1 cup warm water (105° to 115°F)

1 cup unbleached all-purpose flour

DOUGH

3$^{1}/_{2}$ to 4 cups unbleached all-purpose or bread flour

1 teaspoon salt

$^{1}/_{2}$ cup warm water

2 large eggs, beaten

2 tablespoons olive oil

3 ounces grated Parmigiano-Reggiano (about $^{2}/_{3}$ cup)

2 ounces Gruyère, chopped (about $^{1}/_{3}$ cup)

2 ounces grated pecorino Romano (about $^{1}/_{2}$ cup)

2 ounces provolone, coarsely chopped (about $^{1}/_{2}$ cup)

1. To make the starter, sprinkle the yeast over the warm water and whisk until creamy. Stir in the flour. Cover with plastic wrap and leave at room temperature for at least 1 hour or overnight. The mixture will be thick and bubbly. The longer the starter sits, the better the flavor will be. After 24 hours, cover and store the starter in the refrigerator for up to 3 days.

2. In a bowl combine 3½ cups of the flour and the salt. Scrape the starter into the bowl and add the water. Add the eggs and the oil. Stir until a soft dough forms. On a lightly floured surface, knead in the cheeses. Add more flour as necessary for the dough to hold a soft shape without being sticky. Knead 5 minutes, or until the dough is smooth and the ingredients are well combined. Shape the dough into a ball.

3. Oil a large bowl. Add the dough, turning it once or twice to oil the top. Cover with plastic wrap and place the pan in a warm, draft-free place to rise 1½ hours, or until doubled in bulk.

4. Oil a 15 × 10 × 1-inch jelly-roll pan. Place the dough in the pan, stretching and flattening it with your hands until it covers the bottom. Cover with plastic wrap and let rise 1 hour, or until doubled.

5. Preheat the oven to 375°F. Uncover the pan and bake the pizza until crisp and golden, about 35 to 40 minutes. Run a long metal spatula around the edges and under the pizza, since the cheese has a tendency to stick. Slide the pizza onto a rack and let cool slightly before cutting.

wild mushroom and fontina pizza

PIZZA PIEMONTESE / *serves 4*

*O*ur friends Luciana and Alfredo Currado are the owners of Cantina Vietti, one of the finest wineries in Piemonte, in northwestern Italy. Their Barolo, Barbaresco, and Barbera are frequently cited as some of Italy's best wines. One day when we were in their area, they suggested that we meet them at a pizzeria where they had befriended the owner, a Neapolitan who had moved to Piemonte to make his fortune. Alfredo said that he would bring along some of his wines.

Alfredo's idea of "pizza wines" turned out to be magnums of 1961 Barolo, one of the first vintages that he had made as a young man. We felt privileged to be able to drink these rare and magnificent wines with him.

Even the pizzaiolo rose to the occasion. Rather than serving us a classic Neapolitan pizza, he made one topped with local Piemontese ingredients, combining fresh porcini mushrooms and truffle-scented Fontina Valle d'Aosta.

He proved that a food as simple as pizza can be elevated to gourmet fare. Since fresh porcini are difficult to find here, use other flavorful mushrooms instead. Try to find Fontina from the Valle d'Aosta. It is a much better cheese than Fontina made elsewhere.

8 ounces assorted mushrooms, such as white mushrooms,
  shiitake, or oyster
2 tablespoons olive oil
1 garlic clove, thinly sliced
$^1/_2$ teaspoon chopped fresh thyme leaves or a pinch of dried thyme
Salt and freshly ground black pepper
2 tablespoons chopped fresh parsley
$^1/_2$ recipe Basic Dough (page 64)
4 ounces Italian Fontina cheese, rind removed and thinly sliced

1. Wipe the mushrooms with a damp paper towel. Discard the stems of shiitake mushrooms, if used. Cut the mushrooms into thin slices.

2. In a large skillet, heat the oil with the garlic over medium heat. Add the mushrooms, thyme, and salt and pepper to taste, and cook, stirring frequently. When the mushroom liquid has evaporated and the mushrooms are browned, add the parsley. Let cool.

3. Place the dough on a lightly floured surface. With your fingers, stretch and flatten the dough out to a 12-inch circle.

4. Dust a pizza peel or the back of a baking sheet with flour. Place the dough on the peel, shaking it once or twice to make sure it does not stick. If it does, lift the dough and dust the peel or baking sheet with more flour.

5. Spread the cheese slices over the dough, leaving a ½-inch border all around. Top with the mushrooms.

6. Quickly slide the pizza dough onto the tiles or baking stone. Bake the pizza 6 to 7 minutes, or until the edges are puffed and the crust is crisp and golden brown.

7. Remove the pizza to a cutting board. Cut into wedges and serve immediately.

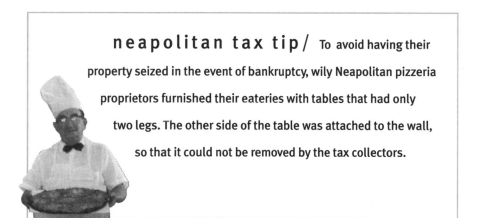

neapolitan tax tip / To avoid having their property seized in the event of bankruptcy, wily Neapolitan pizzeria proprietors furnished their eateries with tables that had only two legs. The other side of the table was attached to the wall, so that it could not be removed by the tax collectors.

sicilian onion and anchovy pizza

SFINCIUNI / *serves 8*

*i*n Palermo, Sicily, a focacceria is an informal restaurant where snack foods are sold. The most famous of these is the Antica Focacceria di San Francesco, which began as a simple takeout shop. At some point, a few marble tables were added and it evolved into a restaurant. One of their specialties is a sandwich called a *vastedda,* made on a soft, round sesame-seed roll filled with *milze,* beef spleen, sautéed in lard and layered with ricotta and grated caciocavallo cheese. It will never replace a Whopper in this country, but the restaurant's patrons love it. Other focacceria specialties are fried foods like *arancine,* crisp balls of rice stuffed with meat sauce and peas; panelle, chickpea fritters; and this delicious pizza made with a puffy dough and an onion, tomato, and anchovy topping.

Brooklyn still has several Sicilian-style focaccerias. Two of our favorites are Joe's Focacceria on Avenue U and Ferdinando's Focacceria on Union Street. Both are very authentic, and Italian Americans come from all over the United States to eat there.

DOUGH

1 package active dry yeast or 2 teaspoons instant yeast

1 cup warm water (105° to 115°F)

About 3 cups unbleached all-purpose flour

1/2 cup grated pecorino Romano

1 teaspoon salt

1/4 teaspoon freshly ground black pepper

2 tablespoons olive oil

1 large onion, thinly sliced

5 tablespoons olive oil

2 cups canned Italian peeled tomatoes with their juice

    or 2 medium tomatoes, peeled, seeded, and chopped

1 teaspoon dried oregano

Salt and freshly ground black pepper

8 anchovy fillets or 1 can (2 ounces), drained and chopped

$^1/_2$ cup bread crumbs made from day-old Italian or French

    bread

$^1/_2$ cup caciocavallo, mild provolone, or ricotta salata,

    cut into $^1/_2$-inch cubes

1. To make the dough, sprinkle the yeast over the water. Let stand until creamy. Whisk with a fork until smooth.

2. In a large bowl, combine the flour, the cheese, and the salt and pepper. Stir in the yeast mixture and the oil. Stir until a soft dough forms.

3. Turn the dough out onto a lightly floured surface and knead until smooth and elastic. Add more flour as necessary if the dough is sticky.

4. Oil a large bowl. Place the dough in the bowl, turning it once to oil the top. Cover with a towel and let rise in a warm, draft-free place until doubled in bulk.

5. To make the topping, cook the onion with 2 tablespoons of the oil in a medium saucepan until tender and golden, about 7 minutes. Add the tomatoes, oregano, and salt and pepper to taste. Cook 10 to 20 minutes, or until the sauce is slightly thickened. Stir in the anchovies. Remove from the heat and let cool. In a small skillet, heat 1 tablespoon oil. Add the bread crumbs and cook over medium heat until toasted and browned.

6. Oil a 12-inch round pizza pan. Place the dough in the pan and stretch and pat it out evenly to fit the pan. Cover and let rise 30 minutes, or until almost doubled.

7. Preheat the oven to 425°F. Uncover the dough and with your fingertips, make dimples by pressing the dough down at 1-inch intervals. Spread half the sauce on the dough, leaving a 1/2-inch border all around. Bake 25 minutes.

8. Spread the remaining sauce on the dough. Scatter the cheese on top and sprinkle with the bread crumbs. Drizzle with the remaining 2 tablespoons oil. Bake 5 to 10 minutes more until the cheese is melted and the pizza is browned around the edges. Cut the pizza into wedges and serve immediately.

riviera chickpea pizza

FARINATA / *serves 6 to 8*

*t*hin pies made with a chickpea flour batter are common in the Mediterranean area, especially along the Riviera. We first encountered them almost thirty years ago while on our honeymoon in Rapallo. The Italians call them *farinate,* while the French name is *socca.* There is also a Sicilian version called *panelle,* where the chickpea batter is allowed to firm up, then cut into small, thin squares and deep-fried instead of baked.

For best results, choose a baking pan with a flat bottom and squared-off edges. The only difficulty in making farinata may be in tracking down the chickpea flour, though most Italian markets can order it for you, and it is widely available through mail order. Do not use Indian-style chickpea flour, which does not have the same flavor or consistency as the Italian kind.

1¹/₂ cups cold water

2 cups chickpea flour

2 teaspoons salt

¹/₃ cup olive oil

About 6 sage leaves, torn into bits

Coarsely ground black pepper

1. Pour the water into a large bowl. Gradually whisk in the chickpea flour. Add the salt and the oil. The mixture should be the consistency of a thin pancake batter. Let stand at least 1 hour at room temperature or covered and refrigerated overnight.

2. Set an oven rack about 5 inches from the source of the broiler heat. Oil a 12 × 9 × 2-inch flameproof pan. Turn on the broiler.

3. Stir the batter again and pour it into the pan. (It should be about ¹/₄ inch thick.) Scatter the sage leaves over the surface and sprinkle with pepper. Place the pan under the heat source. Broil 5 minutes, or until the batter is speckled with brown spots. Reduce the oven heat to 450°F. Bake 5 minutes, or until the farinata is set and it shrinks away slightly from the sides of the pan.

4. Serve hot, cut into squares.

variation   Scatter a few very thin slices of red onion over the top. Substitute chopped fresh rosemary for the sage.

home-style pan pizza

PIZZA ALLA CASALINGA / *makes one 14 x 9-inch pizza*

*W*hen Italians go out to eat pizza, the kind they expect are the thin, plate-size rounds typical of Naples, but pizzas made at home are another story. Homemade pies are thick and baked in a pan like a focaccia, but with more toppings. A farm wife would make one of these pizzas from scraps of dough left after baking the family's weekly bread supply.

A pan pizza has several advantages: It is easier to make than thin-crust pizza, feeds a crowd, and holds up better to reheating. Cut into small squares, it can be served for hors d'oeuvres at parties.

Charles remembers his uncle Joe Sylvester making this pizza on special occasions. Uncle Joe was considered the pizza expert, since his family came from Naples. He learned to make pizza from his grandfather, who owned one of the first pizzerias in the Bronx, on Villa Avenue and 205th Street. It didn't really have a name, just a big sign out front that said Pizzeria. Uncle Joe started with an entire 5-pound bag of flour and baked several pans of pizza at once. The toppings were simple—just cooked ripe tomatoes, mozzarella, olive oil, and garlic—Uncle Joe's personal touch.

Here is a basic recipe for home-style pizza, but use your imagination and add whatever meats, cheeses, and/or vegetables are on hand in the refrigerator—to make it your way. Since the long baking time overcooks the cheese, it is best to add it during the last 5 minutes of cooking.

1 recipe Basic Dough (page 64),
    prepared through step 3
1 recipe Simple Pizza Sauce (page 38), Pizza Maker's
    Sauce (page 67), or sausage and tomato sauce
    (see page 94), about 2½ cups
8 to 12 ounces thinly sliced fresh mozzarella (or use a
    combination of cheeses)
¼ cup grated pecorino Romano or Parmigiano-Reggiano
Olive oil

1. Oil a 15 × 10 × 1-inch jelly-roll pan. With your fist, flatten the dough. Place the dough in the center of the pan and stretch and flatten it out to fit. Cover it with plastic wrap and let it rise about 1 hour until puffy and nearly doubled in bulk.

2. Preheat the oven to 450°F.

3. With your fingertips, firmly press the dough to make dimples at 1-inch intervals all over the surface. Spread the sauce over the dough, leaving a ½-inch border. Bake 20 minutes.

4. Remove the pizza from the oven. Arrange the slices of cheese on top. Sprinkle with the grated cheese. Drizzle with oil. Return the pizza to the oven and bake 5 minutes, or until the cheese is melted and the crust is browned.

focaccia

*f*occaccia is a flatbread that spans the gap between pizza and bread. Sometimes the difference between pizza and focaccia is very slight, and in Italy the names often are used interchangeably. Generally speaking, focaccia toppings are lighter and the crust thicker. In most cases, focaccia is baked in a pan. There are many, many variations.

In Liguria focaccia seasoned with olive oil and salt is served at every meal. In hotels at breakfast, warm slices are included in the bread basket. At midmorning, shoppers and students stop at their local bakery for a hot baked focaccia square. In Puglia crisp focaccia dotted with ripe tomato slices is a favorite antipasto. During the *vendemmia*, or harvest season, bakeries in Tuscany sell a delicious fresh grape focaccia flavored with walnuts and rosemary or honey and black pepper to be eaten with dessert wine or coffee.

Focaccia can be round, square, or rectangular; it can be stuffed or eaten plain. Leftover focaccia, thinly sliced and toasted, makes delicious crackers, known as Genoa Toasts (page 160), to serve with cheese, salads, or soups. In short, focaccia takes on many personalities and appears in different guises throughout Italy. We have even seen cakes that are called focaccia, though this chapter is a collection of some of the more pizzalike versions we have encountered.

To make focaccia ahead, let cool completely on a wire rack. Cut the focaccia into 2 or 4 pieces, whatever size is convenient. Wrap the pieces individually in aluminum foil and freeze them for up to 1 month. To reheat, unwrap the frozen focaccia and place it in a hot oven until lightly toasted, about 10 minutes.

focaccia

serves 8

*M*ost guidebooks to Italy describe Genoa as unsafe and uninteresting. But we found the exact opposite to be true. We loved to walk through the narrow medieval streets, browse in the markets, and gaze at the grand palazzi. Genoa is the city where Christopher Columbus was born in 1451, and where Marco Polo, locked up in prison, dictated his famous book of travels. Though the city was heavily bombed during World War II, there is still much to see and do.

Genoese cooking is excellent, too. They make many special kinds of pasta, including one made with chestnut flour. Delicate pesto, made from basil with the tiniest leaves we have ever seen, is the typical pasta sauce. Genoese cooks are also famous for their sweets and pastries. *Marrons glacés,* candied chestnuts, were invented in Genoa. Our favorite discovery, though, was focaccia, served hot, sprinkled with coarse salt, and infused with luscious green olive oil. It appears at every meal, often topped with herbs or olives or sliced onions. People crowd (Italians never line up) into bakeries, waiting for the focaccia to come out of the oven.

For a thicker focaccia, bake the dough in a 12 × 9-inch pan.

1 package dry yeast
1 cup warm water (105° to 115°F)
6 tablespoons olive oil
About 3 cups unbleached all-purpose flour
2 teaspoons coarse sea salt or kosher salt, plus
    more for sprinkling

1. Sprinkle the yeast over the water. Let stand 1 minute, or until the yeast is creamy. Stir to dissolve the yeast. Add 2 tablespoons of the oil.

2. In a large bowl, combine the flour and the salt. Add the yeast mixture and stir until a soft dough forms. Turn the dough out onto a lightly floured surface and knead until smooth and elastic, about 10 minutes, adding more flour if the dough seems sticky.

3. Lightly coat a large bowl with oil. Place the dough in the bowl, and turn it to oil the top. Cover with plastic wrap. Let rise in a warm, draft-free place until doubled in bulk, about 1½ hours.

4. Oil a 15 × 10 × 1-inch jelly-roll pan. Flatten the dough and place it in the center of the pan. Stretch and pat the dough out to fit. Cover with plastic wrap and let rise about 1 hour until puffy and nearly doubled.

5. Preheat the oven to 450°F. Set the oven rack in the center of the oven. With your fingertips, firmly press the dough to make dimples at 1-inch intervals all over the surface.

6. Drizzle the remaining 4 tablespoons oil over the top. Sprinkle lightly with coarse salt.

7. Bake 20 to 25 minutes, or until golden brown and crusty. Transfer to a rack to cool slightly. Cut into slices and serve warm.

with grated cheese/ Instead of salt, just before baking, sprinkle the focaccia with freshly grated pecorino Romano and ground black pepper.

with olives and thyme/ In step 3, after the dough is kneaded, add 1 cup chopped pitted black or green olives and 1 teaspoon chopped fresh thyme.

with sage and onion/ Scatter 2 tablespoons chopped fresh sage and one thinly sliced onion over the dough just before baking.

focaccia sandwich/ In step 4, place the dough to rise in an oiled 10-inch-round springform pan. Just before baking, sprinkle with coarse salt and rosemary leaves. Bake as directed. With a serrated knife, split the focaccia into two layers. Spread the bottom half with soft goat cheese or robiola. Top with roasted asparagus, red onion rings, and sliced peppers (see Roasted Vegetables, page 188). Replace the top half and cut into wedges to serve.

red onion, goat cheese, and thyme focaccia

serves 8

> 3 ounces goat cheese
>
> Focaccia (page 154) dough, prepared through step 5
>
> 1 red onion, thinly sliced
>
> 4 tablespoons olive oil
>
> 1 teaspoon chopped fresh thyme leaves or ½ teaspoon
>   dried thyme
>
> Salt and freshly ground black pepper

1. Crumble the goat cheese over the focaccia dough. Toss the onion with 2 tablespoons of the oil and scatter them over the dough. Sprinkle with the thyme and salt and pepper. Drizzle with the remaining oil.

2. Bake 25 to 30 minutes, or until golden brown and crusty. Transfer to a rack to cool slightly. Cut into slices and serve warm.

garlic, anchovy, and walnut focaccia

serves 8

*I*n the Piedmont section of northern Italy, this focaccia was called the bread of Charles Albert because it was served to the troops on the occasion of the king of Savoy's visit. It has a most delicious aroma. If you use the salted anchovies that are sold whole in a large tin, it will taste even better.

> 4 garlic cloves, finely chopped
> ¼ cup olive oil
> Salt and freshly ground black pepper
> Focaccia (page 154) dough, prepared through step 5
> 1 can anchovy fillets, drained or 6 salted anchovies prepared
>   as directed on page 7
> ½ cup coarsely chopped walnuts

1. Combine the garlic, oil, and salt and pepper. Brush the mixture over the prepared dough.

2. Cut the anchovies into 2 or 3 pieces and press the pieces into the top of the dough. Scatter the walnuts over the top and pat them in. Bake 25 minutes, or until crisp and golden. Cut into slices and serve warm.

little focaccias

FOCACCINE AL ROSMARINO / *makes 8*

*i*ndividual focaccia buns are perfect for sandwiches stuffed with prosciutto, cheese, grilled or roasted vegetables, hamburgers, tuna salad, etc. Or serve them unstuffed as dinner rolls. The possibilities are endless. You can vary the flavoring with other herbs, chopped onion, or coarsely ground black pepper.

1 package dry yeast

$^1/_2$ cup warm water (105° to 115°F)

1 cup milk

7 tablespoons olive oil

About 3 cups unbleached all-purpose flour

1 cup fine semolina flour

1 tablespoon fresh rosemary leaves, minced

1 teaspoon salt

Additional fresh rosemary leaves or coarse salt

    for the tops

1. In a large bowl, sprinkle the yeast over the water. Let stand for 1 minute, or until creamy. Stir to dissolve the yeast. Stir in the milk and 3 tablespoons of the olive oil.

2. Add the all-purpose flour, the semolina, the chopped rosemary, and the salt. Stir until a soft dough forms.

3. Turn the dough out onto a lightly floured surface and knead until smooth and elastic, about 10 minutes, adding additional flour if necessary.

4. Place the dough in a large oiled bowl. Turn the dough to oil the top. Cover loosely with a towel and let rise in a warm, draft-free place until doubled in bulk, about 1$^1/_2$ hours.

5. Oil two large baking sheets. Punch the dough down to eliminate air bubbles. Divide the dough into 8 pieces. Shape the dough into balls. Flatten the balls out to 4-inch disks. Place the disks about 3 inches apart on the baking sheets. Cover with a towel and let rise about 1 hour until puffy and nearly doubled.

6. Preheat the oven to 400°F. Set the oven rack in the center of the oven. With your fingertips, firmly press the disks to make dimples at 1-inch intervals all over the surface of the dough. Drizzle the remaining 4 tablespoons oil over the tops. Sprinkle lightly with rosemary or salt. Bake 20 to 25 minutes, or until golden. Transfer the rolls to a rack to cool. Serve warm.

the pizza diet/ Scientists have found that people who eat diets rich in both fresh tomatoes and processed tomato products have a reduced risk of many cancers. Lycopene, a powerful antioxidant that gives tomatoes their red color, appears to be responsible. There is one small hitch, however. In order to be effective, lycopene must be eaten with fat, as in vegetable oil or cheese. Don't be surprised then if your doctor prescribes a regular diet of pizza.

genoa toasts

*M*any of the focaccias in this chapter make terrific toasts that you can use in place of crackers or bread. They keep a long time. You can toast any focaccia that does not have moist or perishable ingredients in it. Best choices are Whole Wheat Flatbread (page 172), basic Focaccia (page 154), Golden Focaccia (page 162), Little Focaccias (page 158), or Wine Focaccia (page 174).

1. Cut leftover focaccia into ¼-inch-thick slices. If you like, brush the slices on each side with olive oil and sprinkle with coarse salt. Arrange the slices in a single layer on a baking sheet.

2. Bake in a preheated 300°F oven 30 to 40 minutes, or until very crisp and lightly browned. The slices must be completely dried out or they will not keep.

3. Place on a rack and let cool completely. Store in an airtight container in a cool, dry place.

roman potato focaccia

FOCACCIA DI PATATE ALLA ROMANA / *serves 8*

*O*ne year, when Charles was a teacher, he took a sabbatical and we spent several months touring Italy. In Rome we stayed in a little pensione for a month, and every day we explored the city. We went far beyond the usual tourist haunts and had lots of time to discover old catacombs, out-of-the-way museums, and little-known churches. Most evenings, we would join the locals for dinner at a family-run trattoria near the Piazza di Pasquino, but for lunch one of our favorite haunts was a little takeout pizzeria between the Pantheon and Piazza Navona. Their specialty was thin-crusted Roman-style pizza, which was sold *a taglia,* by the slice. The clerk would cut off a piece or two, weigh it, and charge us accordingly. Our favorite was this crisp, brown-edged potato pie topped with rosemary. We like to use flavorful yellow-flesh potatoes, such as Yukon Gold.

> **1 pound boiling potatoes, such as Yukon Gold (3 to 4**
>   **medium)**
> **Focaccia (page 154) dough, prepared through step 4**
> **Olive oil**
> **Salt and freshly ground black pepper**
> **1 to 2 tablespoons chopped fresh rosemary leaves**

1. Preheat the oven to 425°F. With your fingertips, firmly press the dough to make dimples at 1-inch intervals all over the surface. Set the oven rack in the top third of the oven.

2. Peel the potatoes and slice them very thin. Arrange the potatoes overlapping slightly in neat rows on top of the dough. Brush the potatoes with the oil. Sprinkle evenly with the salt and pepper. Scatter the rosemary on top.

3. Place the focaccia in the oven and bake 30 minutes. Raise the heat to 450°F. Bake 10 minutes more, or until the potatoes are tender and browned on the edges. Slide the focaccia onto a board and cut into slices.

golden foccacia

FOCACCIA D'ORO / *serves 8*

Cornmeal adds crunch and a slightly sweet corn flavor as well as a golden color to this focaccia. Serve it for breakfast or brunch, plain or topped with fresh ricotta (page 13).

> **1 package dry yeast**
> **$^1/_2$ cup warm water (105° to 115°F)**
> **$1^1/_4$ cups milk**
> **$^1/_4$ cup olive oil**
> **About 3 cups unbleached all-purpose flour**
> **1 cup fine yellow cornmeal**
> **1 teaspoon salt**
> **1 teaspoon fennel seeds**
> **$^2/_3$ cup golden raisins**

1. In a large bowl, sprinkle the yeast over the water. Let stand for 1 minute, or until creamy. Stir until the yeast is dissolved.

2. Stir in the milk and oil. Add the flour, cornmeal, salt, and fennel seeds. Stir well until a soft dough forms. Turn the dough out onto a lightly floured surface and knead until smooth and elastic, about 10 minutes. Add more flour if the dough seems too sticky. Knead in the raisins.

3. Place the dough in a large oiled bowl. Turn the dough to oil the top. Cover loosely with plastic wrap and let rise in a warm, draft-free place until doubled in bulk, about 1 hour.

4. Oil a 15 × 10 × 1-inch jelly-roll pan. With your fist, flatten the dough to eliminate air bubbles. Place the dough in the pan, stretching and patting it with your hands to fit evenly. Cover with plastic wrap and let rise until puffy and doubled, about 1 hour.

5. Preheat the oven to 425°F.

6. Uncover and bake until browned and crusty, about 30 minutes. Slide the focaccia onto a rack to cool slightly. Cut into slices and serve warm.

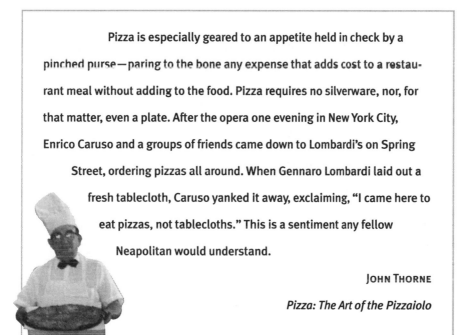

Pizza is especially geared to an appetite held in check by a pinched purse—paring to the bone any expense that adds cost to a restaurant meal without adding to the food. Pizza requires no silverware, nor, for that matter, even a plate. After the opera one evening in New York City, Enrico Caruso and a groups of friends came down to Lombardi's on Spring Street, ordering pizzas all around. When Gennaro Lombardi laid out a fresh tablecloth, Caruso yanked it away, exclaiming, "I came here to eat pizzas, not tablecloths." This is a sentiment any fellow Neapolitan would understand.

JOHN THORNE

Pizza: The Art of the Pizzaiolo

parmesan pepper focaccia

serves 6 to 8

*i*n our kitchen we keep two peppermills, both filled with black peppercorns. The larger mill grinds the pepper fine, which is useful for most cooking purposes. The smaller one grinds the pepper into coarse grains, which we use in this focaccia recipe and other dishes where a pronounced peppery bite is desired. Do not use flavorless ready-ground black pepper.

> **1 package active dry yeast**
> **1 cup warm water (105° to 115°F)**
> **¼ cup olive oil**
> **About 3 cups unbleached all-purpose flour**
> **1 cup freshly grated Parmigiano-Reggiano**
> **2 teaspoons coarsely ground black pepper**
> **1 teaspoon salt**

1. In a large bowl, sprinkle the yeast over the water. Let stand for 1 minute until the yeast is creamy. Stir until the yeast is dissolved. Add the oil and stir well.

2. Add the flour, cheese, pepper, and salt. Stir the mixture until a soft dough forms.

3. Turn the dough out onto a lightly floured surface. Knead until smooth and elastic, about 10 minutes, adding more flour if the dough feels sticky.

4. Oil a large bowl and place the dough in it, turning it once to oil the top. Cover with plastic wrap and let rise in a warm, draft-free place until doubled in bulk, about 1 hour.

5. Oil a 12 × 9 × 2-inch baking pan. Flatten the dough to eliminate air bubbles. Stretch and pat out the dough to fit the prepared pan. Cover loosely with plastic wrap and let rise 1 hour, or until puffed and nearly doubled.

6. Preheat the oven to 450°F.

7. Uncover and bake the focaccia in the center of the oven until golden brown and crisp, about 20 minutes. Slide the focaccia onto a rack to cool slightly. Cut into rectangles. Serve warm.

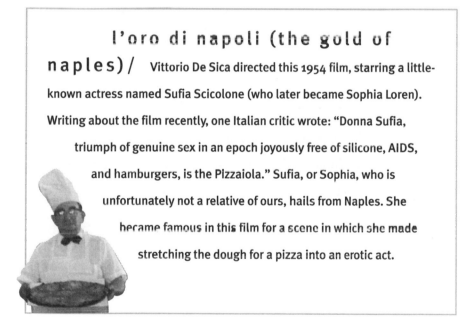

l'oro di napoli (the gold of naples) /
Vittorio De Sica directed this 1954 film, starring a little-known actress named Sufia Scicolone (who later became Sophia Loren). Writing about the film recently, one Italian critic wrote: "Donna Sufia, triumph of genuine sex in an epoch joyously free of silicone, AIDS, and hamburgers, is the Pizzaiola." Sufia, or Sophia, who is unfortunately not a relative of ours, hails from Naples. She became famous in this film for a scene in which she made stretching the dough for a pizza into an erotic act.

tomato and olive focaccia

FOCACCIA DI POMODORI / *serves 8 to 10*

*i*n Apulia focaccia is typically made with semolina flour. Chunks of fresh tomato are pressed into the indentations on the top and oregano is sprinkled over all.

We discovered this tasty variation in Foggia, a city in the northern part of Apulia, where we had gone to visit a wine producer who was conducting some interesting experiments with grape varieties. He was growing Primitivo, a typical Apulian varietal, alongside California Zinfandel to determine if the two grapes are related. When Charles tasted the unlabeled wines made from the two grapes side by side, he immediately recognized which was the Zinfandel and which was the Primitivo. No scientific conclusions were reached that day, but we did enjoy drinking the wines with the fresh-baked focaccia the winemaker offered us.

Mashed potatoes kneaded into the dough make the texture moist and the flavor rich and delicious, while zesty black olives add a salty tang. Since this dough is very soft and sticky, it is best to make it with a heavy-duty mixer.

> 1¹/₂ **pounds baking potatoes, peeled and cut into 1-inch**
>   **chunks (about 2 large potatoes)**
> **1 package active dry yeast**
> **5 tablespoons olive oil**
> **About 4 cups unbleached all-purpose flour**
> **3 teaspoons salt**
> **4 to 5 plum or Roma tomatoes**
> ¹/₂ **cup imported black olives, pitted and coarsely chopped**

1. Place the potatoes in a medium saucepan and add water to cover. Bring to a simmer over medium heat and cook until very tender when pierced with a fork, about

15 minutes. Drain the potatoes, reserving ³/₄ cup cooking liquid. Mash the potatoes by passing them through a ricer or food mill.

2. When the potato water has cooled to lukewarm, about 105° to 115°F, pour it into the large bowl of a heavy-duty electric mixer. (Substitute warm tap water if the potato water is not available.) Sprinkle the yeast over the water. Let stand 1 minute, then stir until the yeast dissolves. With the paddle attachment, stir in the potatoes and 3 tablespoons of the oil.

3. Blend in the flour and the salt. With the dough hook, knead at low speed for 5 minutes, or until the dough is smooth and elastic. The dough should be soft and sticky yet should form a ball. Add additional flour, if needed.

4. Oil a large bowl and scrape the dough into it. Turn the dough to oil the top. Cover with plastic wrap and let rise in a warm, draft-free place until doubled in bulk, about 1¹/₂ hours.

5. Oil a 15 × 10 × 1-inch jelly-roll pan. With your fist, press the dough down. With oiled hands, pat the dough out to fit the pan evenly. Cover loosely with plastic wrap and let rise for 1 hour until doubled.

6. Preheat the oven to 450°F. Cut the tomatoes in quarters lengthwise and scoop out the seeds and juice. Cut the quarters crosswise into ¹/₄-inch-thick slices.

7. Dimple the dough by making deep indentations with your fingertips at 1-inch intervals all over the surface. Scatter the olives over the dough. Press a piece of tomato in each indentation. Drizzle the surface with the remaining 2 tablespoons olive oil.

8. Bake 25 to 30 minutes, or until golden. Slide the focaccia onto a rack to cool slightly. Cut into slices and serve warm.

tuscan crazy bread

PANEPAZZO / *serves 8*

*d*uring the harvest season in Tuscany, very ripe wine grapes are used to make this delicious, lightly sweet focaccia. The flavor of the wine grapes is deeper and more intense than that of table grapes, and the Italians don't seem to mind crunching on the seeds! We like to make this with red seedless grapes, which are always in good supply. Since this bread is somewhat unusual, the Tuscans sometimes call it *panepazzo*, crazy bread, though it makes perfect sense to us.

Charles loves the combination of the slightly sweet bread and hot, plump, juicy grapes. He likes to have it for breakfast with a cup of steaming cappuccino.

Serve this focaccia as a light meal with cheese and salami, or try it with a glass of Vin Santo or other dessert wine. It also goes well with a cup of tea.

¹/₃ cup full-flavored olive oil

2 tablespoons fresh rosemary leaves, chopped

1 package dry yeast

1 cup warm water (105° to 115°F)

3 cups unbleached all-purpose flour

4 tablespoons sugar

2 teaspoons salt

2¹/₂ cups red grapes (about 12 ounces), washed, stemmed,
and thoroughly dried

1 cup coarsely chopped walnuts

1. In a small saucepan, warm the oil over medium heat. Add the rosemary and remove from the heat. Let cool.

2. In a large bowl, sprinkle the yeast over the water. Let stand 1 minute, or until creamy. Stir until dissolved.

3. Add the oil and rosemary, the flour, 2 tablespoons of the sugar, and the salt. Stir until a soft dough forms.

4. Turn the dough out onto a lightly floured surface and knead until smooth and elastic, about 10 minutes, adding more flour if the dough feels very sticky. Shape the dough into a ball.

5. Oil a large bowl and place the dough in it, turning it once to oil the top. Cover with a towel and let rise in a warm, draft-free place until doubled in bulk, about $1^1/_2$ hours.

6. Preheat the oven to 375°F. Place the oven rack in the upper third of the oven. Oil a 15 × 10 × 1-inch jelly-roll pan.

7. With your fist, press the dough down to eliminate air bubbles. Stretch and pat the dough out with your hands to fit the prepared pan. Cover with plastic wrap and let rise about 1 hour, or until puffed and nearly doubled.

8. Scatter the grapes and walnuts evenly over the dough, pressing them in lightly. Sprinkle with the remaining 2 tablespoons sugar.

9. Bake 30 to 35 minutes, or until the focaccia is lightly browned and crisp. Slide the focaccia out of the pan and onto a rack. Serve warm or at room temperature.

pancetta and rosemary focaccia

serves 8

*p*ancetta is made from the same cut of pork as is bacon. Usually, the meat is seasoned with salt and black pepper, though some manufacturers use other seasonings, such as garlic. The meat is then rolled up to resemble a salami and aged. Occasionally, pancetta is also smoked, but this is not typical. If you cannot find pancetta, substitute lean salt pork.

1 package dry yeast

1 cup warm water (105° to 115°F)

2 tablespoons olive oil

4 ounces finely chopped pancetta (about 1 cup)

1 tablespoon chopped fresh rosemary leaves

About 2¹/₂ cups unbleached all-purpose flour

1 teaspoon salt

1. In a large bowl, sprinkle the yeast over the water. Let stand 1 minute, or until creamy. Stir until the yeast is dissolved.

2. Add the oil, pancetta, rosemary, flour, and salt. Stir until a soft dough forms. Turn the dough out onto a lightly floured surface and knead until smooth and elastic, about 10 minutes, adding more flour if the dough feels sticky.

3. Shape the dough into a ball. Oil a large bowl and add the dough, turning it once to oil the top. Cover with plastic wrap and let rise in a warm, draft-free place until doubled in bulk, about 1 hour.

4. Oil a 12 × 9 × 2-inch baking pan. Add the dough and flatten and stretch it out with your hands to fit the pan. Cover loosely and let rise in a warm place about 60 minutes until puffed.

5. Preheat the oven to 425°F.

6. Uncover and bake the focaccia 20 minutes, or until golden brown and crisp. Slide the focaccia onto a rack to cool slightly. Cut into rectangles and serve warm.

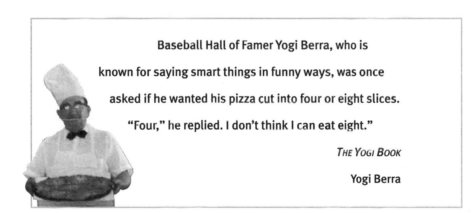

Baseball Hall of Famer Yogi Berra, who is known for saying smart things in funny ways, was once asked if he wanted his pizza cut into four or eight slices. "Four," he replied. I don't think I can eat eight."

THE YOGI BOOK

Yogi Berra

whole wheat flatbread

SCHIACCIATA NERA / *serves 8 to 10*

*O*ur friend Franca Landini always seemed to have this simple focaccia on hand whenever we visited Fattoria Viticcio, the wine estate just outside of Greve in Tuscany, which she and her husband, Lucio, and son Sandro owned. She served us warm slices of flatbread as we sat under the pine trees in the garden and sipped Lucio's Prunaio, a fabulous "super Tuscan" wine.

Schiacciata is the Tuscan name for focaccia. It means flattened or squashed. Whole wheat flour gives this bread a warm, nutty flavor.

1 package dry yeast

³/₄ cup warm water (105° to 115°F)

1 cup milk

6 tablespoons olive oil

About 3 cups unbleached all-purpose flour

1 cup whole wheat flour

1¹/₂ teaspoons coarse or kosher salt, plus more for sprinkling

1. In a large bowl, sprinkle the yeast over the water. Let stand 1 minute, or until creamy. Stir to dissolve the yeast.

2. Add the milk and 3 tablespoons of the oil. Add the all-purpose flour, whole wheat flour, and salt. Stir until a soft dough forms.

3. Turn the dough out onto a lightly floured surface and knead until smooth and elastic, about 10 minutes, adding additional flour if the dough seems very sticky.

4. Oil a large bowl. Add the dough, turning it once to oil the top. Cover with plastic wrap. Let rise in a warm, draft-free place until doubled in bulk, about 1 hour.

5. Oil a 15 × 10 × 1-inch jelly-roll pan. Flatten the dough with your fist. Place it in the center of the pan and stretch and pat it with your hands to fit. Cover with plastic wrap and let rise about 1 hour until puffy and nearly doubled.

6. Preheat the oven to 450°F.

7. With your fingertips, firmly press the dough to make dimples 1 inch apart all over the surface of the dough. Drizzle the remaining 3 tablespoons oil over the top. Sprinkle lightly with coarse salt.

8. Bake 20 to 25 minutes, or until golden brown and crusty. Transfer to a rack to cool slightly. Cut into rectangles and serve warm.

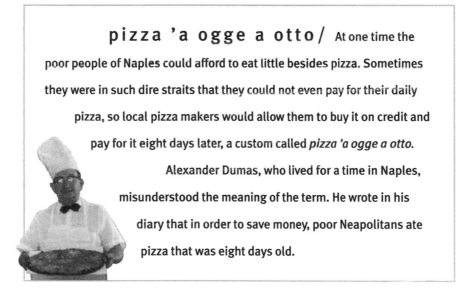

pizza 'a ogge a otto/ At one time the poor people of Naples could afford to eat little besides pizza. Sometimes they were in such dire straits that they could not even pay for their daily pizza, so local pizza makers would allow them to buy it on credit and pay for it eight days later, a custom called *pizza 'a ogge a otto.* Alexander Dumas, who lived for a time in Naples, misunderstood the meaning of the term. He wrote in his diary that in order to save money, poor Neapolitans ate pizza that was eight days old.

wine focaccia

FOCACCIA AL VINO

a starter is a mixture of yeast, water, and flour that is allowed to sit at room temperature for an hour or more. The purpose of using a starter to make dough is to give the focaccia or bread a deep flavor. At first, the starter bubbles up, but it soon collapses. It is then mixed with more flour and additional liquid and turned into a moist, sticky dough. The result is a focaccia that is puffy and light with a great flavor. Use an electric mixer or food processor for this dough, since it is sticky and hard to handle.

STARTER

1 package dry yeast

1 cup warm water (105° to 115°F)

1 cup unbleached all-purpose flour

DOUGH

3 cups unbleached all-purpose flour

2 teaspoons coarse or kosher salt

$^1/_2$ cup sage leaves, torn into small pieces (or use a mixture
   of fresh herbs, such as rosemary, sage, thyme, oregano,
   and basil)

$^1/_4$ cup olive oil

$^1/_2$ cup dry white wine

TOPPING

2 tablespoons olive oil

1 teaspoon coarse sea salt

1. To make the starter, sprinkle the yeast over the water and let stand 1 minute, or until creamy. Stir until the yeast is dissolved. Stir in the flour. Cover with plastic wrap and leave at room temperature for about 1 hour or up to 24 hours. The mixture will be thick and bubbly.

2. To make the dough, in a large mixer bowl with the paddle attachment, or in a food processor fitted with the plastic blade, combine the flour and the salt. Add the starter, sage, oil, and wine. Mix until a soft dough forms. If using an electric mixer, replace the paddle with the dough hook. Knead the dough until smooth and elastic, but it should remain soft and sticky.

3. Oil a large bowl. Add the dough, turning several times to oil the top. Cover with plastic wrap and let rise in a warm, draft-free place until doubled in bulk, about 1^{1}/$_{2}$ hours.

4. Oil a 15 × 10 × 1-inch jelly-roll pan. Flatten the dough with your fist. Place the dough in the pan. Pat and stretch it out with your hands to fit the pan evenly. Cover with plastic wrap and let rise until doubled, about 1 hour.

5. Preheat the oven to 425°F. Press the dough firmly with your fingertips to make dimples about 1 inch apart all over the surface. Drizzle with oil. Sprinkle with salt.

6. Bake 25 minutes, or until crisp and golden. Slide the focaccia onto a rack to cool slightly. To serve, cut into rectangles.

gorgonzola walnut focaccia

FOCACCIA AL GORGONZOLA E NOCI / *serves 8*

*b*lue-veined Gorgonzola is one of our favorite cheeses. Look for imported Italian Gorgonzola, which is available either *piccante* or *stagionato*, sharp or aged, or *dolce,* sweet and mild. Either kind can be used for this recipe.

Teamed with crunchy walnuts, Gorgonzola gives this focaccia a tangy yet mellow flavor. Serve the focaccia with a green salad for lunch, or after dinner with a bunch of sweet grapes.

> 1 package dry yeast
> 1¼ cups warm water (105° to 115°F)
> 2 tablespoons olive oil
> 3 cups unbleached all-purpose flour
> 1 teaspoon salt
> 6 ounces imported Italian Gorgonzola
> ½ cup coarsely chopped walnuts

1. In a large bowl, sprinkle the yeast over the water. Let stand 1 minute, or until creamy. Stir until the yeast is dissolved. Add the oil.

2. Add the flour and the salt. Stir the mixture until a soft dough forms. Turn the dough out onto a lightly floured surface. Knead until smooth and elastic, about 10 minutes, adding more flour if the dough feels very sticky.

3. Oil a large bowl and place the dough in it, turning it once to oil the top. Cover with plastic wrap and let rise in a warm, draft-free place until doubled in bulk, about 1 hour.

4. Oil a 15 × 10 × 1-inch jelly-roll pan. Cut off the rind of the Gorgonzola and mash the cheese coarsely with a fork. On a lightly floured surface, lightly knead the cheese into the dough. The cheese should remain chunky and form streaks. Set the dough aside to rest for 10 minutes.

5. Turn the dough out into the pan. Pat and stretch the dough out to fit the pan. Cover with plastic wrap and let rise in a warm, draft-free place for 1 hour, or until puffy and nearly doubled.

6. Preheat the oven to 400°F. Scatter the walnuts on top of the dough and pat them in lightly.

7. Bake the focaccia in the center of the oven for 25 minutes, or until golden. Slide a metal spatula under the focaccia to loosen it from the pan and transfer it to a cutting board. Cut into rectangles. Serve warm.

MARGHERITA con prosciutto
Pomodoro, Mozzarella, Formaggio e Basilico
MARGHERITA con funghi
Pomodoro, Mozzarella, Formaggio e Basilico
MARGHERITA alla romana
Mozzarella, Acciughe, Pomodoro e Basilico
MARGHERITA con prosciutto e funghi
Pomodoro, Mozzarella, Formaggio e Basilico
MARGHERITA con panna
Pomodoro, Mozzarella, Formaggio, Basilico e Panna
MARGHERITA con filetto pomodorini
Filetto di pomodoro, Flor di latte, Formaggio e Basilico
PIZZA al prosciutto crudo
Pomodoro, Mozzarella, Prosciutto crudo,
Formaggio e Basilico
PIZZA CAPRESE
Pomodoro per insalata, Mozzarella, Basilico ed Origano
PIZZA alla campagnola
Olive, Acciughe, Pomodoro, Capperi, Aglio ed Origano
PIZZA sostanziosa
Pomodoro, Mozzarella, Prosciutto, Uova,
Formaggio e Basilico
PIZZA lasagna
Pomodoro, Mozzarella, Ricotta, Prosciutto, Formaggio e B
PIZZA forte
Salame piccante, Peperoni sottolio, Pomodoro,
Peperoncino e Basilico
PIZZA alle 4 stagioni
Campagnola, Marinaresca, Margherita con funghi
PIZZA capricciosa
Mozzarella, Prosciutto, Pomodoro, Funghi,
Olive, Capperi, Formaggio e Basilico
PIZZA con salsiccia e friarielli

HOTEL SANTA LUCIA
NAPOLI

antipasti and accompaniments

With protein from the cheese, meat, or fish topping and carbohydrates from the tomatoes, vegetables, and crust, a pizza can make a fairly complete and balanced meal. Add a salad and some fruit, and you are really eating healthy, without a lot of fuss.

Of course, there are many other side dishes that go well with pizza. We like to serve all kinds of mixed salads and marinated vegetables, since the vinegar or lemon juice in the dressing makes a good foil for the richness of the pizza. Marinated carrots, mushrooms, eggplants, and beans are all nice complements to a pizza menu.

Also included in this chapter is a classic seafood salad to have with focaccia or to serve as an appetizer before pizza.

aunt loretta's mushrooms

FUNGHI MARINATI / *makes 1 pint*

*O*ne day Michele's aunt Loretta was choosing mushrooms at her Brooklyn greengrocer's when she got into a conversation with another shopper. He told her he was making marinated mushrooms and volunteered the recipe. They sounded so good, she hurried home to try them, and they turned out great. We like them with cold cuts or cheese as an antipasto.

Make the mushrooms about two days before you plan to serve them.

1 package (10 to 12 ounces) mushrooms
1/2 cup white wine vinegar
2 garlic cloves
1 teaspoon salt
1/2 teaspoon dried oregano
Pinch of crushed red pepper
Olive oil, optional

1. Place the mushrooms in a bowl and rinse them quickly in cold running water. Do not let the mushrooms remain in the water or they will become saturated with liquid. Cut off a thin slice from the stem end. If the mushrooms are large, cut them into halves or quarters.

2. In a medium saucepan, bring 1/2 cup water and vinegar to a boil. Add the mushrooms and cook 5 minutes. Remove the pan from the heat. With a slotted spoon, remove the mushrooms to a bowl. Reserve the liquid.

3. Toss the mushrooms with the garlic, salt, oregano, and red pepper. Transfer the mushrooms to a 2-cup glass jar, pressing them down with the back of a spoon. Add enough of the reserved vinegar to cover. Let cool slightly, then cover and refrigerate 24 hours before serving. These keep well for up to 2 weeks.

4. Just before serving, drizzle with a little olive oil, if desired.

beans with mint and garlic

FAGIOLI ALLA MENTA / *serves 6*

*b*eans are such an important and nutritious part of the Tuscan diet that they are often called "the meat of the poor." Chopped mint, garlic, and vinegar give this warm bean salad a tasty spike. You can use either spearmint or peppermint.

> 8 ounces (1 cup) dried cannellini or Great Northern beans
> Salt
> 1/4 cup vinegar
> 1/4 cup extra virgin olive oil
> 1 rib celery, chopped
> 2 whole garlic cloves
> 1/2 cup chopped fresh mint
> Freshly ground black pepper

1. Rinse the beans in cold water and discard any shriveled beans or stones. Place the beans in a bowl with 2 inches of cold water to cover. Refrigerate at least 4 hours or overnight.

2. Preheat the oven to 300°F.

3. Drain the beans and place them in a flameproof casserole with a cover. Add fresh water to cover by 1 inch. Cover and bring just to the simmer over low heat. Place the casserole in the oven and cook until the beans are very tender, about 1 hour and 15 minutes. (Cooking time may vary, depending on the age and size of the beans.) The liquid should just cover the beans. If necessary add a little hot water to the pot. Test several beans by tasting them for doneness, since they may not all be ready at the same time.

4. When the beans are tender and creamy, add salt and cook for 10 minutes more. Do not overcook or the beans may begin to break apart.

5. Drain off most of the liquid and add the remaining ingredients. Stir well. Serve warm or at room temperature.

spicy olive and fennel salad

INSALATA DI FINOCCHIO / *serves 4*

*f*ennel is sometimes called anise, although the two are not the same. The mixup probably comes from the fact that both fennel and anise have a slight licorice flavor. Fennel is delicious eaten cooked or raw. Italians serve wedges of it as part of a dessert fruit course because they believe it aids digestion.

If fresh fennel is unavailable, substitute a combination of celery and carrots in this crunchy salad. It keeps well for up to three days.

1 medium fennel bulb

2 cups large green olives, pitted and sliced

3 garlic cloves, thinly sliced

1/4 cup chopped fresh parsley

Pinch of crushed red pepper

1/4 cup olive oil

2 tablespoons red wine vinegar

Pinch of salt

1. Trim off any brown spots on the fennel and cut a thin slice off the base. Discard the green stems down to the rounded bulb. Cut the fennel in half lengthwise, then into thin slices.

2. In a serving bowl, combine all the ingredients and toss well. Cover and chill 1 hour, or until ready to serve.

roasted marinated eggplant

MELANZANE A SCAPECE / *serves 8*

*t*hough we associate eggplant with Italian cooking, it actually originated in North America and was unknown in Italy until after Columbus.

    This dish tastes better when it is made at least a day or two before
serving it so that all the flavors can come together. If you prefer, you can fry or grill the
eggplant slices instead of roasting them.

> **2 medium eggplants**
> **Salt**
> **About ¹/₂ cup olive oil**
> **4 garlic cloves, very finely chopped**
> **¹/₂ cup finely chopped basil or mint**
> **¹/₄ cup red wine vinegar**

1. Trim the eggplants. With a vegetable peeler or a sharp paring knife, trim off 1-inch
strips of the skin lengthwise all around, giving the eggplants a striped appearance. Cut
the eggplants crosswise into ¹/₄-inch-thick slices. Layer the slices in a colander set over
a bowl, sprinkling each layer with salt. Let stand 30 minutes to 1 hour. Quickly rinse
the eggplant slices under cool water. Pat dry with paper towels.

2. Preheat the oven to 425°F. Brush two large baking sheets with oil. Arrange the
eggplant slices in a single layer on the prepared baking sheets. Bake 20 minutes, or until
lightly browned.

3. Make a layer of eggplant slices in a shallow serving dish. Sprinkle with the garlic,
basil, and vinegar. Repeat layering until all the ingredients have been used. Cover
tightly and refrigerate overnight or up to 3 days. Remove the dish from the refrigerator
about ¹/₂ hour before serving.

green bean and tuna salad

INSALATA DI FAGIOLINI E TONNO / *serves 4*

*t*he waters around Sicily were once abundant with tuna. The fish was so plentiful that the Sicilians figured out a way to can it, something that had never been thought of before. Italians prefer dark-fleshed tuna for canning. It has more flavor and a moister consistency than white tuna.

Charles's cousin prepared this delicious salad for us a few years ago while we were visiting his family in Agrigento. It is best when freshly made, otherwise the beans lose their fresh color and flavors. But you can prepare the beans and cheese ahead, then wrap them and keep them separate. You can even combine the dressing in the bowl. When ready to serve, just whisk the dressing and toss with the remaining ingredients.

1 pound green beans, trimmed

Salt

3 tablespoons olive oil

3 tablespoons fresh lemon juice

1 can (7 ounces) tuna, preferably packed in olive oil

½ cup mild provolone, caciocavallo, or Swiss cheese, cut into narrow strips

2 tablespoons chopped capers

1 tablespoon chopped fresh parsley or basil

Freshly ground black pepper

1. Bring a large pot of water to boiling. Add the beans and salt to taste. Cook 5 to 8 minutes, or until just tender. Drain well and cool under cold running water. Pat the beans dry. Cut them into 1-inch lengths.

2. In a bowl, whisk together the oil and lemon juice and a pinch of salt. Add the beans, tuna, cheese, capers, and parsley, and toss well. Season to taste with pepper.

crunchy carrots

serves 6

*t*hese bright, crispy carrots are just the thing to munch on while waiting for your pizzas to bake. They keep well in the refrigerator for several days. To serve them as a salad, drain off the cooking liquid and toss the carrots with extra virgin olive oil.

1 pound carrots

Sprig each of parsley, rosemary, mint, and basil

1/2 cup dry white wine

1/2 cup white wine vinegar

1 garlic clove

1 tablespoon sugar

1/2 teaspoon fennel seeds

Pinch of salt

1. Peel the carrots and trim the ends. Cut the carrots into quarters lengthwise.

2. Tie the parsley, rosemary, mint, and basil into a bundle with kitchen twine.

3. Place the carrots and the herb bundle in a medium skillet. Add the remaining ingredients and enough water to just cover the carrots. Bring the liquid to a simmer and cook until the carrots are crisp tender, 7 to 8 minutes. Remove the skillet from the heat and let cool. Discard the herbs.

4. Store the carrots and their cooking liquid in an airtight container in the refrigerator. To serve, partially drain the carrots and place them in a serving dish.

sweet-tart peppers

PEPERONI IN AGRODOLCE / *serves 6*

*S*ome people lose all self-control at the sight of a dessert cart, but not Michele. She prefers very simple desserts, like fresh fruit or crunchy biscotti. An antipasto table is another story, however. She can't resist it.

One day we were at Gigino Pizza a Metro (which calls itself the University of Pizza) in Vico Equense, near Naples. It's an enormous restaurant that attracts big families who order their specialty—pizza by the meter—yard-long pies with all kinds of interesting toppings. They also have great seafood, pasta, and antipasto. In fact, Michele was so taken by the antipasto table, she took several photos of it, much to the amusement of a group of diners nearby. Michele got the last laugh, though, when she pried the recipe for these sensational sweet-tart peppers from a friendly waiter. We serve them as an appetizer or as a side dish with grilled sausages or ribs.

4 medium-size red or yellow bell peppers (about 1½ pounds)

1 to 2 jalapeño peppers or other chiles, or a pinch of crushed red pepper

4 garlic cloves, chopped

1 large ripe tomato, cored and chopped

2 tablespoons raisins

2 tablespoons olive oil

1 tablespoon red wine vinegar

1 teaspoon sugar

Pinch of dried oregano

1 tablespoon chopped fresh parsley

1. Preheat the oven to 400°F.

2. Cut the peppers in half lengthwise and remove the stems, seeds, and white membranes. Slice the peppers into 1-inch strips.

3. Oil a 12 × 9 × 2-inch baking and serving dish. Add all the ingredients except the parsley. Toss well. Spread the ingredients in an even layer.

4. Bake 50 to 60 minutes, or until the peppers are tender and lightly browned on the edges.

5. Let cool to room temperature. Sprinkle with parsley.

roasted vegetables

serves 4

*r*oasting vegetables gives them a deep caramelized flavor and rich texture. We can make a meal of them alone, though they are also terrific as a pizza topping (Follonico's Roasted Vegetable Pizza, page 92) or focaccia stuffing. Add other vegetables if you like, such as whole shallots, asparagus, or eggplant.

The most important thing to remember about cooking the vegetables is that the pan must be large enough to accommodate them in a single layer. If they are piled up, the vegetables will steam and become soggy and bland instead of rich and brown. An ideal choice is a 15 × 10 × 1-inch jelly-roll pan. Because it has low sides, the steam escapes easily and the vegetables brown evenly.

1 head of garlic

2 large bell peppers, any color, seeded and cut into wedges

2 medium onions, cut into wedges

2 medium zucchini, scrubbed and cut into 1/2-inch slices

1 medium tomato, cored and cut into wedges

1/4 cup olive oil

Salt and freshly ground black pepper

1. Preheat the oven to 400°F. Break up the garlic into individual cloves. Discard the excess skin, but do not peel the cloves.

2. In a roasting pan large enough to fit all the vegetables in a single layer, toss all the ingredients together. Distribute the vegetables evenly in the pan.

3. Roast 45 minutes to an hour, turning occasionally, until browned and tender. Serve hot or at room temperature.

tuna pâté

PÂTÉ DI MAGRO / *serves 6*

*t*his luscious pâté is easy to assemble when you are pressed for time. It keeps well in the refrigerator for several days. Spread it on Genoa Toasts (page 160) or celery ribs.

> 1 can (7 ounces) tuna in olive oil, drained
> 1 garlic clove
> 1 stick (8 tablespoons) unsalted butter, cut up
> Salt
> 2 to 3 teaspoons fresh lemon juice
> 1 tablespoon chopped fresh parsley

1. Combine the tuna and garlic in a food processor. Chop fine. Blend in the butter, salt, and lemon juice to taste.

2. Line a 2-cup bowl with plastic wrap. Pack the tuna mixture into the bowl.

3. Serve immediately or cover with plastic wrap and refrigerate. To serve, invert the bowl onto a plate and peel off the plastic wrap. Sprinkle with parsley. If the pâté has been chilled, let it soften at room temperature before serving.

seafood salad

ANTIPASTO ALLA MARINARA / *serves 6*

*d*id you know that calamari are shellfish? Their shell is flexible and clear and it is found *inside* the body, not outside like clams or mussels. When you buy cleaned calamari, check them carefully for pieces of plasticlike shell and gelatinous viscera, which are often left behind. Rinse the calamari thoroughly inside and out.

Feel free to vary this salad according to the kinds of shellfish available. You can use one type of seafood or several different kinds. Scallops, clams, or octopus would be good and typically Italian.

The secret to a fresh-tasting seafood salad is to add the dressing in stages, half when mixing the salad and half just before serving.

1 pound mussels, debearded and scrubbed

2 medium potatoes, peeled

1 pound medium shrimp, shelled and deveined

8 ounces cleaned calamari

2 cups sliced mushrooms

1/2 cup sliced green olives

1/4 cup chopped capers

1 small garlic clove, very finely chopped

1/3 cup extra virgin olive oil

About 1/4 cup fresh lemon juice

Salt and coarsely ground black pepper

2 tablespoons chopped fresh parsley

Lettuce leaves

Lemon wedges for garnish

1. Place the mussels in a large pot. Cover and place over medium heat. Cook until the mussels open, about 4 minutes. Remove the mussels from the shells. Strain the mussel juices into a bowl through a paper coffee filter or a double thickness of cheesecloth.

2. Place the potatoes in a large saucepan of water with salt to taste. Cook until tender, about 15 minutes. Remove the potatoes, reserving the water.

3. Add the shrimp to the boiling water and cook 2 minutes, or just until the shrimp turn pink. Remove the shrimp with a slotted spoon. Cool under cold running water.

4. Add the calamari to the saucepan and cook, stirring once or twice, just until they turn opaque, about 30 seconds. Drain and rinse under cold running water.

5. Cut the potatoes into bite-size cubes. Cut the squid bodies crosswise into 1/2-inch rings. Cut the tentacles in half if large.

6. In a large bowl, combine the potatoes, seafood, mushrooms, olives, capers, and garlic. Add some of the reserved mussel juices to moisten. Combine the oil, lemon juice, and salt and pepper. Drizzle half the dressing over the salad and toss well. Cover and refrigerate 1 hour, or until ready to serve.

7. Just before serving, add the parsley and the remaining dressing and toss again. Taste for seasoning, adding more lemon juice if needed. Line a serving platter with lettuce leaves and spoon the salad on top. Garnish with lemon wedges.

MARGHERITA con funghi
Pomodoro, Mozzarella, Formaggio e Basilico

MARGHERITA alla romana
Mozzarella, Acciughe, Pomodoro e Basilico

MARGHERITA con prosciutto e funghi
Pomodoro, Mozzarella, Formaggio e Basilico

MARGHERITA con panna
Pomodoro, Mozzarella, Formaggio, Basilico e Panna

MARGHERITA con filetto pomodorini
Filetto di pomodoro, Fior di latte, Formaggio e Basilico

PIZZA al prosciutto crudo
Pomodoro, Mozzarella, Prosciutto crudo,
Formaggio e Basilico

PIZZA CAPRESE
Pomodoro per insalata, Mozzarella, Basilico ed Origano

PIZZA alla campagnola
Olive, Acciughe, Pomodoro, Capperi, Aglio ed Origano

PIZZA sostanziosa
Pomodoro, Mozzarella, Prosciutto, Uova
Formaggio e Basilico

PIZZA lasagna
Pomodoro, Mozzarella, Ricotta, Prosciutto, Formaggio e

PIZZA forte
Salame piccante, Peperoni sottolio, Pomodoro,
Peperoncino e Basilico

PIZZA alle 4 stagioni
Campagnola, Marinaresca, Margherita con funghi

PIZZA capricciosa
Mozzarella, Prosciutto, Pomodoro, Funghi,
Olive, Capperi, Formaggio e Basilico

PIZZA con salsiccia e friarielli

HOTEL SANTA LUCIA
NAPOLI

wine with pizza

$\mathcal{V}$initaly is an enormous wine fair held every April in Verona in the Veneto region of northern Italy. Winemakers from all over Italy set up booths, and professionals in the wine trade and press from all over the world come to sample the current vintages and discuss the wines. Our late friend, Sheldon Wasserman, author of *Italy's Noble Red Wines* (Macmillan, 1991) and many other important books on wine, attended the fair every year. Sheldon, who was quite a character, would walk around the fair carrying his own spittoon. Professional winetasters like Sheldon do not drink the wines they sample, they merely taste them, then discreetly spit them out. This way, they can taste many wines without becoming inebriated. Sheldon prided himself on the huge number of wines he could taste, then take down careful, accurate, and legible notes on all of them. Michele remembers arriving at the fair one day around noontime only to meet Sheldon, who proudly announced that he had already tasted more than three hundred wines in the preceding day and a half! Then he pulled out his notebook and began to tell her all about them.

Sheldon loved pizza and maintained that the best wine to drink with it was champagne. Many Italians feel that pizza goes best with sparkling beverages—including wine, beer, soda, and water.

We appreciate sparkling wines with our pizza, too, but enjoy other wines as well with our pies. The wines in the following list are excellent and reasonably priced (most are about $10 or less) and we enjoy drinking them with all types of food.

Italians often drink beer with pizza. Some Italian brands to look for are Moretti and Peroni.

sparkling wines

These wines complement any pizza.

name	producer
Prosecco	Nino Franco, Foss Marai
Brut Spumante	Ferrari, Rotari

white wines

Serve these wines with vegetable and seafood pizzas.

name	producer
Vernaccia di San Gimignano	Cecchi and Riccardo Falchini
Breganze di Breganze	Maculan
Orvieto Secco	Tenuta Le Velette, Antinori
Galestro	Antinori
Mastro Bianco	Mastroberardino
Soave Classico	Anselmi
Pinot Bianco	Alois Lageder, Rivera
Libaio	Ruffino
Leverano Bianco	Conti Zecca
Vigna dei Pini	D'Angelo
Pinot Grigio	Castelcosa, Enofriulia, Di Lenardo

red wines

Serve these wines with cheese and meat pizzas.

name	*producer*
San Giovese di Toscana	Cecchi
Chianti Classico	Castello di Gabbiano, Isole e Olena, Geographico, Viticcio
Rosso	Monte Antico
Rubesco	Lungarotti
Salice Salentino	Cosimo Taurino, Vallone
Ciró Rosso	Librandi
Rubizzo	Rocca della Macie
Cannonau	Sella and Mosca
Santa Cristina	Antinori
Regaleali Rosso	Regaleali
Rosso Conero	Umani Ronchi
Montepulciano d'Abbruzzi	Masciarelli
Perdera Monica di Sardegna	Argiolas
Chianti Montalbano	Capezzano
Barbera d'Asti	Michele Chiarlo
Barbera d'Alba	Vietti

Pizzeria TRIA

NAPOLI · Via Pietro Colletta n. 42/44/46
Tel. (081) 553.94.26

ORDINAZIONE № 0290

TAVOL

MARINARA	
Aglio, Origano, Pomodoro e Basilico	
MARINARA con vongole	
Aglio, Origano, Pomodoro e Prezzemolo	
MARGHERITA	
Pomodoro, Mozzarella, Formaggio e Basilico	
MARGHERITA con uovo	
Pomodoro, Mozzarella, Formaggio e Basilico	
MARGHERITA con prosciutto	
Pomodoro, Mozzarella, Formaggio e Basilico	
MARGHERITA con funghi	
Pomodoro, Mozzarella, Formaggio e Basilico	
MARGHERITA alla romana	
Mozzarella, Acciughe, Pomodoro e Basilico	
MARGHERITA con prosciutto e funghi	
Pomodoro, Mozzarella, Formaggio e Basilico	
MARGHERITA con panna	
Pomodoro, Mozzarella, Formaggio, Basilico e Panna	
MARGHERITA con filetto pomodorini	
Filetto di pomodoro, Fior di latte, Formaggio e Basilico	
PIZZA al prosciutto crudo	
Pomodoro, Mozzarella, Prosciutto crudo	

S A G L I E R A

Brandi®
La pizza... dal 1780

EL SANTA LUCIA
NAPOLI

our favorite pizzerias and restaurants

Polistina's
2275 Broadway
New York, New York

The Spot
163 Wooster Street
New Haven, Connecticut

Tra Vigne
1050 Charter Oak Avenue
St. Helena, California

Tribeca Grill
375 Greenwich Street
New York, New York

i Trulli Restaurant and Enoteca
122 East 27th Street
New York, New York

naples, italy
Ciro a Santa Brigida
Via Santa Brigida, 71-74

Da Ettore
Via Santa Lucia, 56

Da Matteo
Via Tribunali, 94

Da Michele
Via Cesare Sersale, 1-3

Lombardi a Santa Chiara
Via Benedetto Croce, 59

Pizzeria Brandi
Salita Sant'Anna di Palazzo, 1-2

Pizzeria Trianon
Via Pietro Colletta, 42-46

acknowledgments

We received help, tips, recipes, encouragement, advice, and inspiration for this book from many, many sources. Though we were not always able to record the names of the Neapolitan pizzaioli who we watched and learned so much from as they went about their work, we offer them our heartfelt thanks. They patiently answered our questions, demonstrated their techniques, and smiled for our photos.

We would also like to thank Chris Bianco, Ciro Verde, Nicola Marzovilla, Dora Marzovilla, Brad Bonnewell, Tony Montalto, Salvatore Esposito, Tony May, Alan Tardi, John Mariani, Umberto Damiano, Nunzio Castaldo, the Conti Zecca, Loretta Balsamo, Joe Sylvester, Millie Castagliola, Dr. Robert LaRusso, Frieda Rennet, Kevin Benvenuti, Don Pintabona, and Tony Di Dio for their contributions. The International Olive Oil Council, Oldways Preservation and Trust, and the Italian Trade Commission organized several excellent research trips and provided us with a wealth of information.

Special thanks to Harriet Bell, our editor at Broadway Books, and Judith Weber, our agent, who together cooked up the idea for this book after hearing Michele describe Charles's fascination with pizza as she taught a cooking class at De Gustibus at Macy's.

Roberto de Vicq de Cumptich at Broadway Books contributed much to the design of our book. Thanks, also, to designer Barbara Balch for giving the book its stylish appearance, to copy editor Sonia Greenbaum for carefully reading and editing our words, and to Broadway's Caitlin Connolly, Lisa Bullaro, and Alexis Levenson for their assistance.

With patience and understanding for our recipes, Ellen Silverman took the enticing photos, which do so much to enhance this book. Rory Spinelli styled the food so that the photos look good enough to eat.

mail order sources

The Baker's Catalogue
P. O. Box 876
Norwich, Vermont 05055-0876
1-800-827-6836
flour, yeast, equipment

Balducci's Shop from Home Service
P. O. Box 10373
Newark, New Jersey 07193-0373
1-800-BALDUCCI or 225-3822
Fax: 718-786-4125
Web site: www.balducci.com
mozzarella curd, mozzarella di bufala,
cheeses, prosciutto, salami, semolina flour,
olive oil

The Mozzarella Company
2944 Elm Street
Dallas, Texas 75226
1-800-798-2954
fresh mozzarella and ricotta

Sur La Table
84 Pine Street
Seattle, Washington 98101
1-800-243-0852

Williams-Sonoma
P. O. Box 7456
San Francisco, California 94120
1-800-541-2233

bibliography

Anderson, Burton, *Treasures of the Italian Table*, New York: Morrow, 1994.

Antonares, Alfredo, "La Regina Napoletana," *Gambero Rosso*.

Behr, Edward, "Pizza in Naples," *The Art of Eating*, Peacham, Vermont, Spring 1992.

Benincasa, Gabriele, *La pizza napoletana*, Napoli: Alfredo Guida Editore, 1992.

Corriher, Shirley, *Cookwise*, New York: Morrow, 1997.

Field, Carol, *Focaccia*, San Francisco: Chronicle Books, 1994.

Jenkins, Steven, *Cheese Primer*, New York: Workman, 1997.

Killeen, Johanne, and George Germon, *Cucina Simpatica*, New York: HarperCollins, 1991.

Leader, Daniel, and Judith Blahnik, *Bread Alone*, New York: Morrow, 1993.

Ludovisi, Orietta Boncompagni, *Pizza Supremo Sfizio*, Rome: L'InsorGente Editore, 1996.

Massa, Nunzia, ed., *Napoli Guide*, Naples: Graphotronic Edizioni, 1994.

Perna, G. R., *Pizze & C.*, Rome: Edizioni Polaris, 1994.

Prandi, Raffaela, "Pizza: Air, Water and Fire," *Gambero Rosso*.

Romer, Elizabeth, *Italian Pizza and Hearthbreads*, New York: Clarkson N. Potter, 1987.

Sloman, Evelyne, *The Pizza Book*, New York: Times Books, 1984.

Stuller, Jay, "As American as Pizza Pie," *Smithsonian* magazine, June 1997.

Thorne, John, *Pizza: The Art of the Pizzaiolo*, Boston: The Jackdaw Press, 1991.

index